WEAPON

BRITISH SNIPING RIFLES SINCE 1970

STEVE HOUGHTON
Series Editor Martin Pegler

Illustrated by Johnny Shumate & Alan Gilliland

OSPREY PUBLISHING
Bloomsbury Publishing Plc
Kemp House, Chawley Park, Cumnor Hill,
Oxford OX2 9PH, UK
29 Earlsfort Terrace, Dublin 2, Ireland
1385 Broadway, 5th Floor, New York, NY 10018, USA
E-mail: info@ospreypublishing.com
www.ospreypublishing.com

OSPREY is a trademark of Osprey Publishing Ltd

First published in Great Britain in 2021

A catalogue record for this book is available from the British
Library.

ISBN: PB 9781472842350; eBook 9781472842367;
ePDF 9781472842336; XML 9781472842343

21 22 23 24 25   10 9 8 7 6 5 4 3 2 1

Index by Rob Munro
Typeset by PDQ Digital Media Solutions, Bungay, UK
Printed and bound in India by Replika Press Private Ltd.

Osprey Publishing supports the Woodland Trust, the UK's
leading woodland conservation charity.

To find out more about our authors and books visit
www.ospreypublishing.com. Here you will find extracts, author
interviews, details of forthcoming events and the option to sign
up for our newsletter.

Unless otherwise credited, all photographs are from the author's
collection.

Front cover, above: The L115A3 Long Range Rifle. (Author's
collection)

Front cover, below: © Osprey Publishing.

Title-page photograph: Snipers prepare to fire their L115A3 rifles
on Salisbury Plain. Note the Leupold tactical spotting scope in
the foreground and the short tactical suppressor fitted to the
fourth rifle in. (Image by Stuart A Hill AMS; © Crown copyright
2017)

CONTENTS

INTRODUCTION

In the mid-1950s, after the conclusion of the Korean War (1950–53), the British Army ended its selection and training of men for sniper duties; the training facilities at Llanberis, Hythe and Bisley closed and the most skilled and proficient of riflemen ceased to ply their trade. Although the sniper had more than proved his worth during World War II and the Korean War, once again – as was the case after World War I – sniping within the British Army would fall foul of punishing cuts implemented by the War Department, pressed to make savings wherever it could find them. The future for this highly skilled rifleman once again looked vulnerable.

The cleaving of Germany into east and west at the end of World War II created a divide that laid the foundations for a new kind of conflict; the threat of all-out war with the Soviet Union and its Warsaw Pact allies was constant and training for it was rigorous. The Cold War saw the British Army prepare for future conflict by establishing battlegroups equipped with main battle tanks and armoured personnel carriers, ready to meet and counter any Soviet/ East German invasion. A concentrated effort was applied to playing out futuristic mechanized combat scenarios on the next perceived battleground, West Germany, to both drill the troops involved and as a show of strength to the Soviets, who were always watching and listening. The next kind of war-fighting in which the British Army anticipated being involved would be highly mobile with considerable firepower being brought to bear. The strategy of future war-fighting initially saw no requirement for sniping in this new and modern theatre of battle.

In addition to the British Army's Cold War involvement, however, there would be during this period of cessation other skirmishes, such as the Aden Emergency (1963–67) and the eruption of The Troubles in Northern Ireland in the late 1960s. In these theatres, troops on the ground

OPPOSITE
The Enfield No. 4 Mk 1 (T) rifle, which first emerged in 1941, saw over 30 years of service with the British Army until finally being retired in the early 1970s after its conversion to a 7.62mm sniping rifle. The example pictured is wearing a full American black-walnut wood set and is dated 1944. The last 50 years of British military sniping history have certainly been eventful and have witnessed the disappearance of one great name which for well over a century has been synonymous with the British Army's service rifle: Enfield. While the story of the last Enfield bolt-action rifle's development as a sniping and service weapon through to its demise is intriguing, the story of its replacement by a futuristic, world-beating concept is fascinating.

found there was a gap in their skill sets and they quickly realized the disadvantages of not having access to a sniper – an asset which of course they no longer had. The World War II-vintage .303in Enfield No. 4 Mk 1 (T) sniping rifle was still available, however, with many thousands of complete equipment sets sitting refurbished in stores. In response to these small-scale deployments, the Enfield No. 4 Mk 1 (T) was issued to individuals who completed a brief pre-deployment sharpshooter course. The course was more or less a basic introduction to the rifle and its No. 32 telescopic sight, which had just 3× magnification and a 20mm objective lens; but it was by no means comparative to the sniper training the men who originally carried the same rifles received during World War II and the Korean War.

The status quo was set: for the next two decades the British Army deployed the No. 4 Mk 1 (T) as and when a given situation required it, in the hands of nothing more than a sharpshooter. It would not be until the early 1970s that professional snipers would once again be reintroduced to the ranks of the Army, but before this could be realized there was much catching up to do, as by this time there were no individuals remaining with any sniper-training experience. The Army turned to the Royal Navy for a solution.

The Royal Marines were firmly under the command of the Royal Navy and had their naval heritage to thank for escaping the axe that was wielded through the Army, disbanding all sniper activities in the respective units. Throughout this time the Royal Marines were allowed to continue to run a demanding sniper-selection course. Never having ceased sniper training, the Royal Marines therefore were the only element of the British armed forces capable of deploying trained snipers and as such they used them to great effect in Northern Ireland.

The Royal Marines were naturally therefore tasked with training the Army's future sniper instructors at CTCRM (Commando Training Centre Royal Marines) near Lympstone, Devon, in 1972. This busy period at CTCRM created a nucleus of men who would revive sniping within the British Army by establishing Sniper Wing at Warminster, Wiltshire. At Warminster, a tough six-week course was devised in 1973 to train the men selected and put forward by each infantry battalion as its respective sniper instructor at unit level, and who would usually run the battalion's sniper platoon.

The success of Sniper Wing relieved the additional training pressure on CTCRM and within a year it was self-sufficient and was additionally training special-forces candidates at a second facility established at Blair Atholl, Perthshire, specifically for SAS (Special Air Service) and SBS (Special Boat Squadron) students. This second facility ran throughout the 1970s until special-forces units brought their sniper training inhouse and completely under their own control.

The infrastructure to train and employ snipers was once again established within the British Army. The future for this, the most individual of skills, looked encouraging as every infantry battalion re-formed a sniper platoon. The sniper platoons now needed an effective sniping rifle to do their deadly work.

DEVELOPMENT
Sniping-rifle evolution

ADOPTING THE 7.62×51mm NATO CARTRIDGE

The .303in rimmed (left) and 7.62×51mm NATO rimless cartridges are pictured side by side. Although 7.62×51mm NATO ammunition was first introduced in the 1950s, it is still fully employed throughout NATO today.

As part of the British Army's post-war overhaul, which saw infantry units become exclusively mechanized to fight in conjunction with a heavy presence of tanks, these same units received a new infantry rifle, the 7.62mm L1A1 SLR (Self-Loading Rifle), which replaced the Enfield No. 4 bolt-action rifle within regular infantry battalions. The L1A1's adoption in 1954 saw the British Army begin to abandon its longstanding association with the .303in cartridge. By this time Britain had been a member of NATO (North Atlantic Treaty Organization) for almost a decade and was committed to the logistical unification of a single small-arms calibre. The US-developed 7.62×51mm rimless cartridge became the standard shared cartridge within NATO, a logistical feat which was intended to ease the logistical burden of keeping multiple member states in the fight, had it come to that. The newly adopted L1A1 SLR was at this point used exclusively by the British Army's front-line infantry units. Britain's commitment to the use of the new rimless cartridge meant, though, that *all* British Army units required a personal weapon that used it; but to arm rear-echelon, Territorial and Commonwealth units with the L1A1 SLR as well as front-line infantry units would be an expensive undertaking.

In the early 1960s, a move to arm all the British Army units supporting the main infantry body was granted government approval, which involved plans for stocks of the Enfield No. 4 rifle to be converted to use the 7.62×51mm NATO rimless cartridge. RSAF (Royal Small Arms Factory) Enfield in London began the conversion work, designating the ambitious programme L8A1, which was also extended to include the No. 4 Mk 1 (T). A number of No. 4 Mk 1 (T) rifles were removed from stores, each firing a test group for post-conversion comparison. The conversion from No. 4 Mk 1 (T) to L8A1 (T) required a new barrel and magazine; this involved alteration of the wooden forend, which had to be further machined to accommodate the shape of the new magazine housing. The wartime work undertaken by the famous gunmaking company Holland & Holland of London and which related directly to the conversion of the No. 4 rifle's receiver to sniping configuration was untouched, and outwardly the L8A1 (T) looked largely no different from its previous No. 4 Mk 1 (T) guise, the new magazine which housed the new rimless cartridge being the only real aesthetic giveaway.

The L8A1 (T) rifles were test-fired as 7.62mm-calibre weapons and were found to be completely inaccurate: the batch of No. 4 Mk 1 (T) rifles that had been converted fired test groups which did not relate at all to the test groups the same rifles fired as .303in weapons. Furthermore, this small batch of rifles converted to L8 specification were all inconsistent to each other during test firing. The converted No. 4 rifles intended for general infantry use performed marginally better, but the results were so slight in comparison to the same rifle in .303in calibre that the conversion to 7.62mm calibre was effectively pointless. The RSAF Enfield L8A1 programme was a failure and as such was abandoned in the mid-1960s, resulting in the L1A1 SLR being further issued across the British Army and leaving the venerable No. 4 Mk 1 (T) stranded in the .303in calibre for the foreseeable future.

At about the same time as RSAF Enfield was working on the failed L8A1 programme, the Soviet Union unveiled a new sniper system of its own, the SVD Dragunov. The Dragunov was a scoped, 7.62×54mm-calibre, self-loading, gas-operated weapon designated 'Marksman Rifle' by the Soviets, and was introduced specifically for long-range engagement on the battlefield. This new weapon in the arsenal of the Soviet Union, coupled with the obsolete .303in ammunition issue with the World War II-vintage No. 4 Mk 1 (T), may well have provided some impetus within the British Army to have a sniper system that used the 7.62×51mm NATO ammunition, but cost rather than the armed forces' requirements continued to be at the forefront of British government thinking. At this point it was difficult to see a cost-effective way forward that would result

The L42A1 (above) and L1A1 (below) pictured together. The L1A1 SLR was Belgian in origin, derived from the 7.62mm FN FAL (Fusil Automatique Léger, Light Automatic Rifle), and it first entered British Army service in 1954. These two rifles would do a lot of work together during the L42A1's service, not just in Northern Ireland but more generally, as the L1A1 was the spotter's personal weapon. Note the comparable length of the two weapons.

in an effective 7.62mm NATO sniping rifle, particularly after the embarrassing L8A1 (T) episode. In retrospect it is now clear that in the latter half of the 1960s, the MoD (Ministry of Defence) was moving towards the re-establishment of a sniping capability within the British Army. Moreover, the Soviets had perhaps dispelled any idea that sniping had no part to play in a largely mechanized conflict. Accordingly, the final years of the 1960s saw real momentum build in the effort to arm the British Army's infantry units with a new 7.62mm sniping rifle.

THE L42A1 RIFLE

Origins

In the latter years of the 1960s, the British Army's ITDU (Infantry Trials and Development Unit) at Warminster actively collaborated with the British NRA (National Rifle Association) as it had not gone unnoticed that the latter organization's competitive shooters were enjoying a huge amount of success with the No. 4 action in conjunction with the 7.62×51mm cartridge – the same combination RSAF Enfield had not itself been able to convert successfully earlier in the decade. The NRA's competitive civilian shooters were building rifles centred on the No. 4 action with heavy, free-floating barrels of various lengths and rifling twist-rates. The forends of their rifles were 'sporterized', each being cut down just in front of the stock band to aid the free-floating barrel, which had to be contactless with any part of the forend wood so as not to interfere with the harmonics of the barrel when the rifle was fired.

In 1969, RSAF Enfield took several No. 4 Mk 1 (T) rifles from stores and carried out a conversion that created a rifle that resembled those used by NRA members. The changes made for a very different-looking rifle, with the forend wood being cut down 1.27cm in front of the stock band, thus exposing the barrel and giving it a sporting-rifle appearance.

The L42A1 converted from the No. 4 Mk 1 (T) took on a sporting-rifle appearance thanks to its shortened forend. The example illustrated has a black-walnut buttstock, ash wood cheek rest and beech wood forend and handguard. The forend is a Mk 2 retro-converted to Mk 1 specification, having long lost its original walnut forend and handguard. This particular example is dated 1943 on the wrist, so it almost certainly saw combat use in World War II as a No. 4 Mk 1 (T). The rifle also carries a 1971 conversion date.

Internally, the forend was further machined to accept the heavy, free-floating barrel and the new ten-round box magazine. The new magazine utilized was that originally produced for the L8A1 (T) rifle and lasts as the only tangible evidence that the failed L8A1 programme ever took place, its 1965-dated markings standing as testament to the programme. Holland & Holland's wartime work on the No. 4 rifle's receiver in order to make it compatible with the weapon's telescopic sight was untouched; the telescopic sight remained the No. 32, but it was recalibrated for the trajectory of 7.62×51mm NATO ammunition.

These trial rifles were designated XL42E1 ('XL' denoting experimental status and '42E1' denoting the specification) and were handed over to ITDU for testing and evaluation in small batches with 144-grain (9.33g) L2A2 7.62mm ball ammunition manufactured at ROF (Royal Ordnance Factory) Radway Green, Cheshire. RSAF Enfield's records show that a total of 30 No. 4 Mk 1 (T) rifles underwent conversion to the XL42E1 specification in a relatively short period of time, with the batches supplied all wearing different-specification barrels as ITDU tested different barrel lengths and rifling twist-rate combinations so as to arrive at the optimal specification that would successfully fulfil British Army sniper doctrine in all conditions.

In August 1970, the bolt-operated and newly converted sniping rifle, designated the L42A1, entered service with the British Army. The design and trialling process which led to the final specification entering production was rapid, only having started in the previous year.

The heavy, free-floating barrel

In a short period during 1969 the .303in No. 4 Mk 1 (T) rifle had been transformed, now resembling a 7.62mm sporting rifle rather than the British Army's earlier sniping rifles. ITDU completed their trial, recommending for service a heavy cold-hammer-forged, match-grade barrel, 27.5in (69.9cm) in length, with four rifling grooves in a 1-in-12in right-hand twist-rate, which meant the bullet completed one full rotation in the barrel as it passed along 12in (30.5cm) of its length. The hammer-forging process of these initial barrels left a curious pattern on each barrel's outer surface, which has been said to look like 'snakeskin'. These barrels were expensive to produce and are largely found on L42A1s carrying a 1970 or 1971 conversion date. In the early 1970s the expensive, hammer-forged, fully tapered barrels were replaced with an alternative barrel which was cheaper and easier to produce; these new barrels are largely known by the name of their rifling, which differed from the Enfield rifling in that the internal and external corners that formed the rifling cuts were rounded rather than square, and were produced on machinery incapable of producing a continuous tapered profile, which is what made the original L42A1 barrel expensive. The 'Chordal' barrels were recognizable by a step in the barrel's profile, visible just as the barrel emerged from the forend. The first half of the barrel, from the chamber end to the step, was cold hammer-forged; the second half, from the step to the muzzle, was machined.

The L42A1's sights

The L42A1 provided the sniper with back-up sights as well as a primary telescopic sight. The back-up sights remained the Mk 1 leaf sight fitted to the No. 4 rifle by Holland & Holland during its original No. 4 Mk 1 (T) conversion during World War II. Rather than replacing the rear sight at this juncture with something that could be used at incremented distances,

THE L42A1 REVEALED

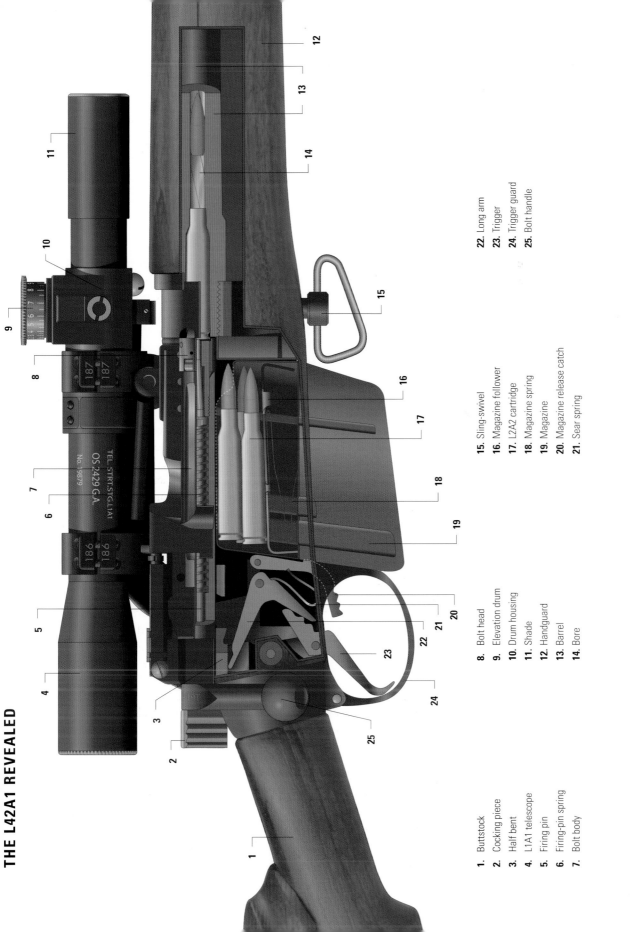

1. Buttstock
2. Cocking piece
3. Half bent
4. L1A1 telescope
5. Firing pin
6. Firing-pin spring
7. Bolt body

8. Bolt head
9. Elevation drum
10. Drum housing
11. Shade
12. Handguard
13. Barrel
14. Bore

15. Sling-swivel
16. Magazine follower
17. L2A2 cartridge
18. Magazine spring
19. Magazine
20. Magazine release catch
21. Sear spring

22. Long arm
23. Trigger
24. Trigger guard
25. Bolt handle

as it was previously when calibrated to 174-grain (11.28g) .303in Mk VII ammunition, it was decided to keep it with an adjustment to the graticule marker lines on the slider which would better suit 7.62×51mm L2A2 ammunition.

The new positions of the slider's graticule marker lines took advantage of the 7.62×51mm round's flatter trajectory, which by zeroing the rifle at 400m and with the slider set at 400 would deliver a hit on a man-sized target between 200m and 500m. A bold letter 'M' was engraved on the slider to denote that it had been modified to metric. The front battle-sight arrangement remained the same as that of the No. 4 Mk 1 (T) rifle's earliest Holland & Holland specification, consisting of a split barrel block band with a female dovetail that received a male-dovetailed front-sight blade which was secured in the block band when the screw at the front of the assembly was tightened. The forward battle sight was completed with a No. 4 rifle's Mk 2 front-sight protector; in order to fit the L42A1 barrel, this required a small section of the barrel at the muzzle to be reduced in diameter, enabling the Mk 2 protector to slide on and be secured with a single screw.

The reticle of the L1A1 telescopic sight remained the 'post-and-wire' pattern, unchanged from its World War II format. This style of reticle had been typical of British sniping optics since 1915.

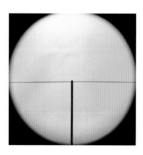

TELESCOPE STRAIGHT SIGHTING L1A1, NSN 1240-99-963-2063	
Manufacturer	Alex Kershaw & Son
Length	11in (27.9cm)
Weight in the mount	2lb (0.9kg)
Objective lens diameter	19mm
Field of view	9°
Magnification	3×
Reticle	Post and wire
Range graduations	100–1,000yd (91–914m)
Focus capability	Fixed
Sunshade	No
Lateral adjustment	16–0–16 MOA
Mount type	Double

The robust No. 32 telescopic sight remained, still permanently captured in its World War II-vintage mounting bracket; only Mk 3 models of the scope were modified to the L1A1 specification, however. The No. 32 Mk 3 was equipped with both a windage and an elevation drum for correction of the bullet's path. The elevation drum was modified to make any corrections align with L2A2 ammunition. As with the back-up sights, once the elevation-drum modification was complete it was marked with a bold letter 'M' to denote metric modification. The L1A1 scope retained the 'post-and-wire' reticle, unchanged from its No. 32 specification.

The L1A1 telescopic sight is pictured with its leather lens caps fitted and in the mounting bracket in which it is permanently held; note that the mounting bracket carries the L42A1's serial number to prevent rifle and scope becoming separated. Also note that the scope is dated 1945.

THE L96A1 RIFLE

A meeting of minds

In the early 1970s, just as the L42A1 was beginning its career, two competitive civilian shooters who were members of the same rifle club, Dave Walls and Dave Caig, represented their countries – England and Scotland respectively. Outside of shooting, both men were precision engineers and although they did not know it themselves at the time, their meeting of minds was to change the world of military sniping forever. The

FAR LEFT
The forward battle-sight assembly slides on to a reduced-diameter section of the L42A1's barrel, mainly to accommodate the No. 4 Mk 1 (T) rifle's World War II-vintage Mk 2 front-sight protector. Note the screw at the front of the assembly; when tightened, it fixes the front-sight blade in place after zeroing by compressing the split block band in which the front-sight blade sits.

LEFT
This close-up of the elevation and windage drums of the L1A1 scope shows the markings for correction. Also note the bold letter 'M' on the elevation drum denoting that metric modification is complete, and the hollow nipple left of the letter 'M'. This latter feature allowed the correction-marked scale ring around the drum to be slipped back to zero after the rifle was zeroed. The scale ring could be pushed left or right by using the tip of a bullet in the hollow nipple.

'two Daves', as they were referred to by their shooting colleagues, recognized that precision competition rifles needed to change from what was largely the norm in the 1970s to something radically different if the boundaries of accuracy were to be pushed, so they began to design and introduce features to their rifles that would improve their performance in competition.

The two Daves' skill in shooting, coupled with their engineering backgrounds, made for a unique partnership that attracted club members who approached them for rifle-smithing work, particularly the fine-tuning of their rifles before competition. The partnership of Dave Walls and Dave Caig was about to be enhanced further when the Olympic competitive shooter Malcolm Cooper joined forces with the duo. Malcolm owned a gun shop in Portsmouth, Hampshire, called Accuracy International Shooting Sports Ltd; having heard of the two Daves' reputation, he met them and soon began to pass all his rifle-smithing work to them. The relationship grew and after seeing their work at first hand, Malcolm suggested that the two Daves should design a rifle: they responded by saying that they already had. The design drawings sat rolled up in a drawer in Dave Walls' house. The features the two Daves had developed up to that point were now all incorporated in one rifle. With the 1978 World Shooting Championships in Seoul, South Korea, on the horizon, Malcolm asked the two Daves to build him the rifle so he could compete with it. They set about realizing the design and produced the rifle Cooper used to win silver in the 50m Rifle Three Positions event.

Cooper's success galvanized the three men, who in the same year formed a new company, Accuracy International Ltd (hereafter AI). AI continued to develop innovative ideas which Cooper put on the world stage with his high-profile competition shooting, but the company's real break was about to occur in the most unforeseen of circumstances. The April–June 1982 conflict which followed the Argentine invasion of the Falkland Islands laid bare the shortcomings of the L42A1 and proved to be the catalyst for change. Although time had been called on the weapon, its complete withdrawal from service with the British Army would take several years. Cooper learned of the British Army's plan to find a replacement sniper system and arranged a meeting with the MoD, which informed him of a future planned trial that would select the new platform and agreed that AI could submit a rifle for consideration. AI set about doing something that had never been done before for the British Army, in that the company set out to design a rifle specifically for the task of sniping; all weapons previously employed in that role by the British Army had been modified service rifles.

The PM Rifle

The rifle designed by AI was at the cutting edge of small-arms design and completely innovative, breaking away from traditional ideas of how a rifle should be built. AI's creation centred on an alloy chassis to which

everything else attached, including two polymer 'skins', or stock sides, which formed the rifle's stock by coming together around the chassis; they were secured by eight long screws which passed through the chassis to fix into the opposite stock side. AI's all-green creation was christened the PM (Practical Marksman) Rifle.

AI completed the PM Rifle in 1984, a year before the MoD trial was scheduled to begin, and used the surplus time to good effect by supplying a small batch of the new rifles to the Royal Marines' SBS, which carried out its own trial and appraisal of the weapon. The PM Rifle was well received, so much so that the British Army's SAS ordered a large quantity of them in the following year, just before the 1985 trial. The special-forces feedback prompted several minor alterations of the weapon before it was submitted. The PM Rifle now sat next to some of the biggest names in the small-arms manufacturing business such as Parker-Hale, Remington, Heckler & Koch and SIG Sauer.

The 1985 trial commenced and quickly saw one competing design after another rejected, leaving just Parker-Hale's M85 and AI's PM Rifle to battle it out for final selection. The Parker-Hale M85 was designed by the company's head armourer Eddy Taff and was built specifically for the trial. It sported several unique features, such as the rear collapsible battle sight that sat beneath the one-piece telescopic-sight mount, as well as being synthetically bedded into a composite stock manufactured by McMillan Fiberglass Stocks, Inc. of Phoenix, Arizona. The accuracy of the M85 was comparable to that of the PM Rifle, matching its 85 per cent probability of hitting a man-sized target at ranges between 600m and 900m: this presented a tough choice to the School of Infantry (redesignated the Land Warfare Centre in 1988) at Warminster. The adjudicators were split, but the PM Rifle was ultimately the victor, carried through by its unique, futuristic design, based as it was on an

The PM Rifle depicted here is of Special Air Service specification, fitted with a black Schmidt & Bender 12×42mm telescope. Note the action, body and barrel, painted green at the regiment's request. The all-green appearance the SAS specified for their own unit-purchased rifles would be a feature carried through to the L96A1 rifle. Also note the bipod's lightweight legs; these would be made more robust for the L96A1.

The Parker-Hale M85 rifle is pictured with the McMillan jungle-camouflage stock, one of five camouflage patterns available. The telescopic sight is the same 6×42mm Schmidt & Bender scope as the L96A1's L13A1; this example even has the same reticle. As with the stock, Parker-Hale offered a choice of several telescopic sights to purchasers of the M85. Although the rifle was not adopted officially by the MoD, it did see service with the British Army, being privately purchased by several units. The serial number was hand-engraved on the bolt handle.

alloy chassis system which addressed the logistical issues currently hampering the service life of the L42A1. At the time, if an L42A1 repair issue could not be rectified by the unit armourer, the rifle had to be packed in its transit chest with all CES (Complete Equipment Schedule) items and then shipped to a command workshop for repair, leaving the unit deficient of a sniping rifle for a period before a replacement rifle arrived. The PM Rifle was set to change this convoluted process as all of its parts were easily attached to the chassis with no specialist skills required to fit them. This meant that the unit could order a new part and the unit armourer could fit it; in fact, the sniper himself was issued with three Allen keys and a single small screwdriver as part of the rifle's CES equipment. These very basic tools meant that the sniper could – with the exception of the barrel – strip down the PM Rifle to all its component parts within several minutes, giving him unprecedented access to his weapon for maintenance and cleaning.

The barrel selected for the PM Rifle was 25in (63.5cm) long and had four rifling grooves with a 1-in-14in (35.6cm) right-hand twist-rate. The barrel also had a green paint finish which matched the receiver, telescopic sight and stock sides; it was supplied by several manufacturers, including Border Barrels, Maddco and Lothar Walther.

The PM Rifle's sights

Like the L42A1, the PM Rifle provided the sniper with a primary telescopic sight backed up by battle 'iron' sights. The L13A1 telescopic sight was in keeping with the rest of the rifle, being supplied in matching green by the manufacturer, the German optics company Schmidt & Bender. The fixed 6× scope had a 42mm-diameter objective lens and like the L1A1 telescopic sight featured both windage and elevation drums that were adjusted in MOA (minutes of angle). The elevation drum also offered the sniper BDC (bullet-drop compensation): a second set of numbers – 1–10 – around the upper half of the drum

acted as quick distance referencing that worked in conjunction with L2A2 ammunition.

Designated the L13A1, the all-green PM 6×42mm telescopic sight was extremely robust. It is illustrated held in its mounting bracket, which – as with the L42A1 – had two large thumbwheel screws for secure fitting to the L96A1. The lens caps are fitted and are the type with transparent lenses.

L13A1 TELESCOPE, NSN V5/1240-99-967-4564	
Manufacturer	Schmidt & Bender
Length	13in (33cm)
Weight with mount	1.17lb (0.5kg)
Objective lens diameter	42mm
Field of view	7m at 100m
Magnification	6×
Reticle	Post and wire
Elevation graduations	100–1,000m
Bullet-drop compensation	Yes
Focus capability	Yes
Parallax adjustment	No
Sunshade attachment	No
Lateral adjustment	16–0–16 MOA
Mount type	Single

The post-and-wire reticle of the L13A1 telescopic sight is illustrated on the range at 300yd (274m). The target is a Figure 14 target; note the level of magnification the 6× scope has at this distance compared to the landscape outside of the scope. It has to be said that hitting a Figure 14 target at this distance was no challenge for the L96A1.

The back-up battle sights were extremely well engineered and very accurate in their own right. Offering 10 MOA windage adjustment in either direction, the rear sight adjusted out to 700m and was collapsible under the L13A1 scope. The forward battle sight slid onto the barrel, which had its diameter reduced at the muzzle end much like that of the L42A1 and the M85.

A doubtful future

In March 1985, much to the company's surprise, AI was awarded an MoD contract to supply 1,112 rifles plus spare parts. The MoD-selected PM Rifle was designated the L96A1 for service, the weapon now sporting this designation on the left-hand side of the receiver. Completed L96A1s were function-tested by Dave Walls and Dave Caig before being delivered to COD (Central Ordnance Depot) Donnington central stores in Shropshire. AI manufactured the first 50 L96A1s which were all supplied to special-forces units, after which the MoD transferred the manufacture of the rifle to Pylon Engineering Ltd of Dartford, Kent. While Pylon Engineering was on the MoD's books as a manufacturer of missiles and ordnance parts, however, the company had no background in the manufacture of small arms. Fully function-tested L96A1s were beginning to reach their intended units when disaster struck. Rifles out on the range were experiencing firing-pin failure, which involved the component breaking just in front of the cocking piece and out of the sight of the sniper. The concealed breakage led to the sniper cycling the bolt as normal with a broken firing pin protruding from the bolt face; when the bolt pushed the new round of ammunition into the chamber, the broken firing pin detonated the round before the bolt could be pushed into the closed position. This led to several injuries and as such the L96A1 was immediately withdrawn from service.

The all-green L96A1 pictured in full military service specification as of 1985. As one can see, the rifle is – apart from one or two physical differences – essentially the same weapon as the PM Rifle illustrated earlier. It was, however, the PM Rifle's successor, the L96A1 sniping rifle, that initiated ground-breaking change to British military sniping doctrine as well as future weapon design.

At this point a military future for the L96A1 looked doubtful, as many critics from various corners of the military who were never in favour of this chassis-based rifle to begin with poured scorn on the weapon and its revolutionary concept. Proposed solutions to the firing-pin problem began to be offered, with calls for the L96A1 to be scrapped and replaced by the Parker-Hale M85. ITDU also began to run trials with the L13A1 telescopic sight mounted on the L42A1 as a quick solution should the issue be drawn out for a prolonged period, and had a bespoke mounting bracket manufactured for the purpose of carrying the all-green scope and attaching it to the L42A1. Ultimately, however, none of this was necessary. AI took control and established that Pylon Engineering had strayed from the materials specification and produced the firing pins in an incorrect steel incapable of withstanding the loads applied to it during function. In addition to the firing-pin issue, AI detected a further fault during their inspection of recalled rifles: two of the four screws that attached the receiver to the top of the chassis were over-bored into the bolt-housing chamber. These holes presented the MoD with a difficult choice – either to scrap the receiver or to fill the holes with a specialist compound. Owing to cost, the MoD agreed to the latter action, which entailed adding a 'C' suffix to the serial number of the affected rifles, indicating concession to the specification.

Following the initial withdrawal of the L96A1 from service and through all the doubts cast over its future, AI resolved the rifle's manufacturing issues swiftly, putting it back in the hands of snipers in just six weeks. The L96A1 went on to serve the British Army as its sniper system for over 25 years, receiving an upgrade starting in 2000, at the halfway point in its service. Enemies on the battlefield developed a healthy respect for the L96A1 and as such it became a much-loved weapon among the men who used it and who honoured it with the epithet 'Green Meanie'.

THE L96A1 EXPOSED

7.62×51mm L96A1

1. Butt spacers
2. Firing pin
3. Rear battle sight
4. L13A1 telescope
5. Forward battle sight
6. Bipod
7. Handguard
8. Hand stop and sling-swivel
9. Mid sling-swivel
10. Magazine
11. Trigger guard
12. Trigger
13. Rear sling-swivel
14. Adjustable support spike
15. Butt pad
16. Sear actuator
17. Sear
18. Sear spring
19. Cocking piece
20. Firing-pin spring
21. Firing pin
22. Bolt
23. Round in chamber
24. Rounds in magazine
25. Magazine follower
26. Magazine spring
27. Magazine release
28. Trigger spring
29. Trigger/sear adjustment screw
30. Pistol grip

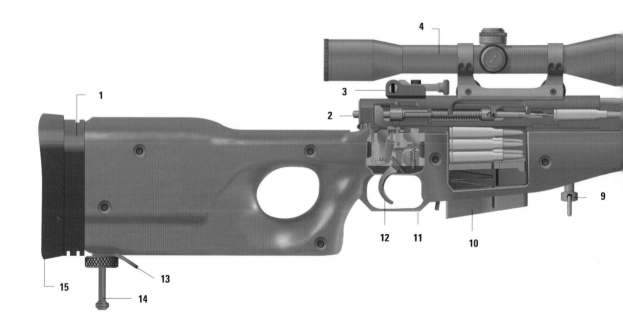

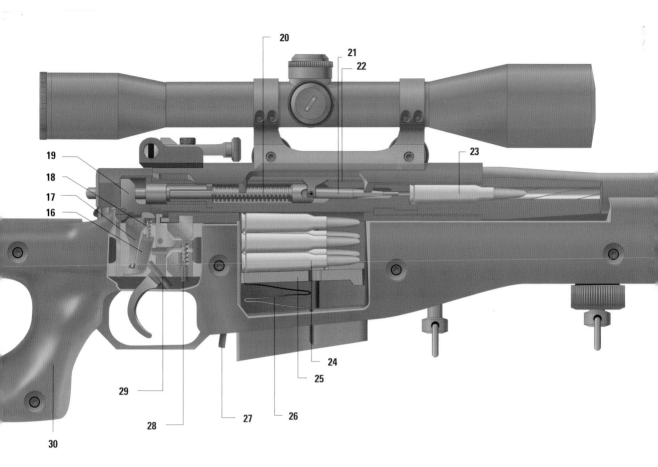

The L96A1 stripped down to all of its component parts. This level of disassembly was achieved in just several minutes with the use of three Allen keys and the single small screwdriver from the weapon's own CES. The image illustrates how unserviceable parts could be changed without fuss or difficulty.

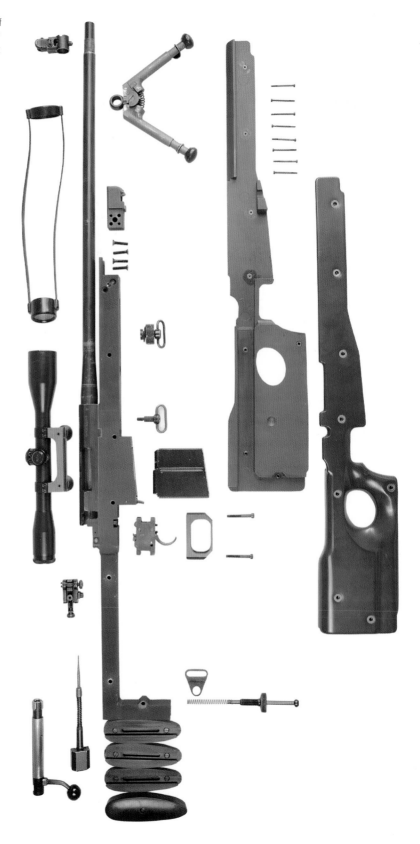

Arctic Warfare: the next generation

The success of the L96A1, or rather the chassis system upon which it was built, had very obvious advantages regarding the ongoing maintenance of a fleet of sniping rifles. The replacement of worn-out parts could not be any simpler and – in contrast to its L42A1 predecessor – to a large extent eliminated the lengthy process an unserviceable rifle had to undergo to become serviceable again. The decision to persevere with the L96A1 during the rocky beginnings of its military service was now paying off for both the British military and AI. While the former enjoyed the benefits deriving from an extremely versatile weapon system that provided unprecedented accuracy as well as fluidity in the logistical upkeep of the weapon, for the latter the now-proven concept of a chassis-based weapon was drawing the attention of military buyers from further afield.

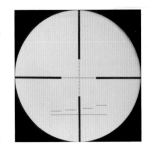

The P4 reticle is a US Marine Corps-designed system that carries a series of mildots on a crosshair pattern. The reticle can be used to determine the distance to a target by measuring the target with the mildots. The sight picture also has within it a set of horizontal stadia lines for bracketing a man from waist to head at set ranges. This reticle design was the first British sniper scope in service in eight decades to break away from the standard post-and-wire design.

The next generation of AI's military sniping rifle would be heavily influenced by the Swedish Army, which approached AI in about 1990. The Swedish Army's request was for a chassis-system rifle based on the L96A1 which had to be capable of operating faultlessly in sub-zero winter conditions. The challenge was accepted by AI, which set about building prototype weapons to test at the US Army's CRTC (Cold Regions Test Center) at Fort Greely, Alaska. The CRTC provided harsh-to-extreme real-world conditions which allowed the prototype weapons to be truly tested, revealing several issues in the original design that required correction. Issues were identified with the stock's thumb hole, the bolt handle and the magazine, all of which received modifications to accommodate a sniper wearing winter gloves. The freezing conditions of the CRTC also exposed a bolt-freezing issue, which resulted in the modification of the bolt body just in front of the handle where the bolt chamber of the receiver completely shrouded it. To overcome the bolt becoming frozen solid in the receiver, the bolt's own body received cuts to its circumference; and it was decided to cast the handle as part of the bolt body instead of attaching it after the bolt body had been manufactured, which was the case with the L96A1.

L17A1 TELESCOPE, NSN B5/1240-99-911-6011	
Manufacturer	Schmidt & Bender
Length	440mm
Weight with mount	1.2kg
Objective lens diameter	50mm
Field of view	11.1–3.4m
Magnification	3–12×
Reticle	Mildot with ranging
Elevation graduations	100–1,000m
Bullet-drop compensation	Yes
Focus capability	Yes
Parallax adjustment	50m to infinity
Sunshade attachment	Yes, plus Killflash
Lateral adjustment	6–0–6mrad
Mount type	Single

The 3–12×50mm Schmidt & Bender PM telescopic sight was designated the L17A1. This example sits in a lever-operated quick-detachable mount as used on the L118-series rifles. The scope was launched on the L118A1 but was also adopted for the L96A1 at the same time as part of that weapon's midlife upgrade. Illustrated with the scope is its sunshade and Killflash filter. Note also the lens caps fitted, which were of the type with clear lenses.

The brute strength of the cast bolt handle, coupled with the cuts in the bolt body which decreased the surface area available to freeze, made operating an iced-up bolt easy and eliminated the issue among troops who operated in sub-zero environments.

In addition, the new rifle had many of the L96A1's proven parts upgraded, such as the resin stock sides, which were very fragile when removed from the L96A1. This fragility was overcome by manufacturing them from a more flexible polymer. In fact, all parts were manufactured from either a corrosion-resistant material, or were treated to a tough protective finish; furthermore, the engineering was so precise that all parts were interchangeable with those of another rifle. In 1991, the Swedish armed forces purchased 1,100 of these new .308in/7.62mm specialist cold-climate rifles, christened the AW (Arctic Warfare) by AI.

The AW rifle now represented the minimum standard being offered to AI's customers, with an order to come from the MoD in subsequent years for the same rifle, albeit with several enhancements including an upgraded telescopic sight. The British Army's adoption of the AW rifle was designated the L118A1. Receiving the designation L17A1, the new rifle's

3–12×50mm Schmidt & Bender PM telescopic sight had parallax adjustment and a 50mm-diameter objective lens. When first introduced with the L118A1, the L17A1 was the first British sniper scope in eight decades to break away from the traditional post-and-wire reticle. Instead, the L17A1 came with a US-style mildot reticle with bracketing stadia lines that measured a man from waist to head at 400m, 600m, 800m and 1,000m. The L17A1 still offered the BDC system on the elevation drum, but now graduated in milliradians (mrad) rather than MOA as per the L13A1. Britain's military initially ordered 48 L118A1s, which were solely for special-forces units and remain in service at the time of writing. The A1 has since been joined by an L118A2 model sporting Dave Caig's folding stock as well as a fully suppressed conversion kit. Among the special-forces personnel that use them, the L118A1 and A2 models are known as the CTSR (Counter Terrorism Sniper Rifle) and CR (Covert Rifle).

THE L115A3 RIFLE

The AW rifle would go on to represent a range of calibres built to the same specification and it would be this platform that AI would choose to develop around the .338in Lapua Magnum cartridge after close cooperation with the Finnish ammunition manufacturer. The mid-1990s saw the AW rifle emerge in the .338in Lapua calibre, branded AWSM (Arctic Warfare Super Magnum); it was swiftly adopted by the MoD, first being issued to special-forces units as the L115A1, as well as to SFSG (Special Forces Support Group). In Iraq and later in Afghanistan, SFSG used the L115A1 to deadly effect out to distances the then-current .308in/7.62mm L96A1 could not

THE L115A3 UNVEILED

.338 L115A3 Long Range Rifle

1. Rear sling-swivel
2. Adjustable cheek rest
3. Butt release catch
4. L24A1 telescope
5. SIMRAD mount
6. STIC Picatinny mount siderail
7. Muzzle brake
8. Bipod
9. Bipod camber lock
10. Hand stop and sling-swivel
11. Magazine

12. Trigger guard
13. Trigger
14. Pistol grip
15. Adjustable support spike
16. Butt spacers
17. Butt pad
18. Sear
19. Sear spring
20. Cocking piece
21. Bolt shroud
22. Firing-pin spring

23. Firing pin
24. Bolt
25. Handguard
26. Round in chamber
27. Large cocking cam
28. Magazine follower
29. Magazine spring
30. Magazine release
31. Trigger spring
32. Trigger/sear adjustment screw

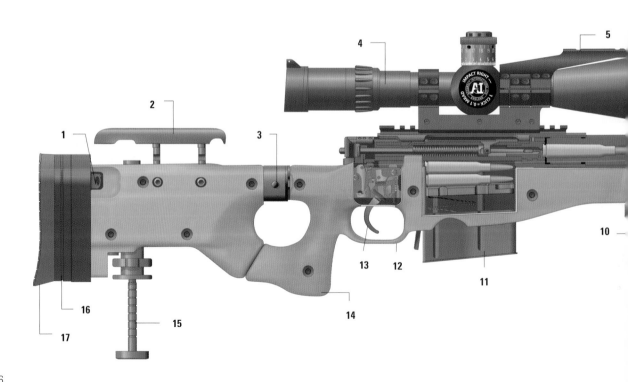

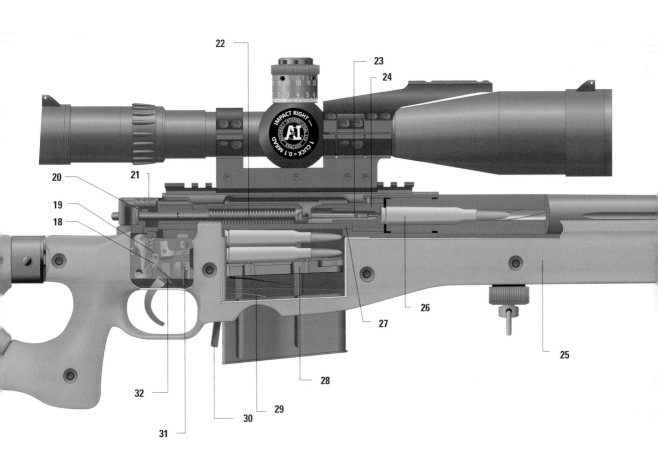

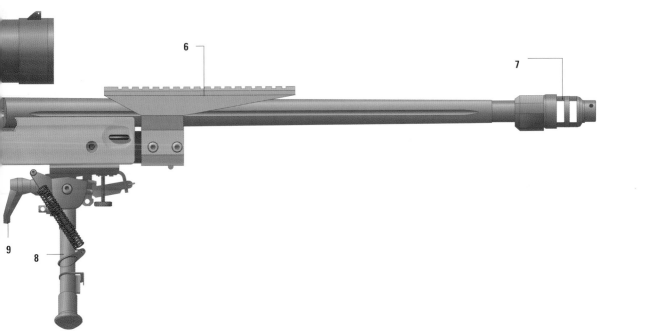

The L24A1 scope is permanently held in a detachable mount, which also has a second mount attached for the SIMRAD night-vision device. The scope's elevation drum has just two complete rotations: the upper set of numbers in yellow around the drum denote that the second rotation is in operation.

match. The L115A1 subsequently became the L115A2 specification, which incorporated a folding stock and a modified bipod.

In 2007 the MoD announced the SSIP (Sniper System Improvement Programme), which was largely dictated by events on the ground in Afghanistan. The SSIP would be the biggest overhaul of the sniper's equipment in British sniping history, let alone since the adoption of the L96A1, which at the time was still the British Army's current sniper system. The British Army planned a huge leap from a .308in/7.62mm sniping weapon to a .338in Super Magnum weapon, which would double the effective deadly sniping range overnight. That year, AI beat off competition from Prairie Gun Works of Winnipeg, Canada to win an MoD contract to supply the L115A3 Long Range Rifle; the first L115A3s were delivered in 2008 and were deployed to Afghanistan immediately, where they met all expectations. The rifle's telescopic sight, designated the L24A1, was still manufactured by Schmidt & Bender like its predecessors. The 5–25× L24A1 had a 56mm-diameter objective lens; the reticle remained the same as for its L17A1 predecessor and was held in a detachable mount incorporating a bracket for mounting the Norwegian SIMRAD night-vision

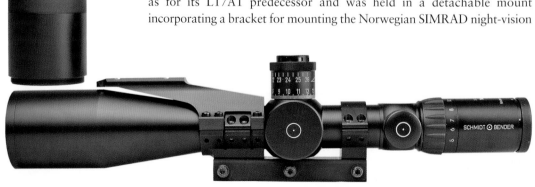

device, which was also delivered as part of the SSIP. The L115A3 had no provision for back-up sights and to date has never been issued with them.

The L115A3 came with a heavy, stainless-steel fluted barrel, 27in (68.6cm) long, with a 1-in-11in (27.9cm) twist-rate; a double-chamber muzzle brake allowed the sniper to screw on a short tactical suppressor. The fluted barrel is unique to the L115A3 as it was developed in conjunction with the 250-grain (16.20g) L4A1 cartridge that has since become the 252-grain (16.33g) Swiss-P cartridge manufactured by RUAG Ammotec AG of Switzerland. On average, the barrel's life extends to about 6,000 rounds in conjunction with a good cleaning regime.

L24A1 TELESCOPE, NSN 1240-99-455-1353	
Manufacturer	Schmidt & Bender
Length	417mm
Weight with mount	1.4kg
Objective lens diameter	56mm
Field of view	5.3–1.5m
Magnification	5–25×
Reticle	Mildot with ranging
Elevation graduations	14mrad per turn
Bullet-drop compensation	No
Focus capability	Yes
Parallax adjustment	Yes
Sunshade attachment	Yes, plus Killflash
Lateral adjustment	6–0–6mrad
Mount type	Single

USE
The long road to sniping excellence

THE L42A1 ENTERS SERVICE

The Metropolitan Police trial

As of late summer 1970, with the commissioning of the L42A1 for service, RSAF Enfield immediately commenced the conversion of World War II-vintage No. 4 Mk 1 (T) sniping rifles to the new specification. Production of the first of the newly produced rifles, of which there were about 30, was completed on 7 December 1970; all carried a conversion date of that same year. Instead of proceeding to COD Donnington central stores prior to entering military service, however, they went straight into a Metropolitan Police trial just one week after their completion, being delivered by road on 14 December.

On receipt the police armourers conducted an intake inspection of the rifles and are on record in their conclusions as being less than impressed, citing numerous faults. It was noted that for all of the weapons, the breech bolt head was fouling the magazine platform; and all of the rifles had badly fitting magazines. For seven of the rifles, full-scale adjustment of the scope was not available. The front pads were loose for five rifles, while five had loose screws in the cheek rest; for four weapons, both the handguards and the front lands were loose. Other faults relating to one weapon in each case included: a split cheek rest; a burr on the front pad; the butt being out of alignment; the slide on the rear sight being sticky; the striker being loose; the back-sight scale being blurred; the rear sight fouling the breech charger guide; and the front-sight protector being loose.

The police armourers requested that RSAF Enfield send its own inspection team to Old Street Station, London, to investigate the faults; this occurred in January 1971. RSAF Enfield's own report

RIFLE 7.62MM L42A1, NSN B1/1005-99-963-3786	
Calibre	7.62mm
Magazine capacity	10 rounds
Overall rifle length	46.5in (118.1cm)
Barrel length	27.5in (69.9cm)
Twist-rate	Four-groove, right-hand 1-in-12in (30.5cm)
Combat weight	12lb (5.4kg)
Iron sights	Graduated to 1,300yd (1,189m)
Conversion approval date	24 August 1970
Converted by	RSAF Enfield
Scope mounted	Over bore
Quantity converted	c.1,100

noted that the vast majority of the faults were within specification and were flagged by the police armourers because of their inexperience with the standards specified for the conversion programme, coupled with their inexperience as to the method of back-up and telescopic sight adjustment. The police armourers clearly had a much higher expectation and were at odds with RSAF Enfield, each party standing by its own interpretation of the standard. With this, the Metropolitan Police terminated the trial; this action is corroborated by the weapons next appearing in RSAF Enfield's own log as being delivered to COD Donnington central stores in January 1971, after which if they entered service it was almost certainly with the Royal Marines as the British Army was still two years away from establishing Sniper Wing at Warminster. The Royal Marines were the first to take receipt of the new L42A1 rifle, which they used not only to train the fledgling British Army instructors, but also operated alongside their .303in No. 4 Mk 1 (T) rifles until the older weapons' final demise in about 1973. Indeed, the Royal Marines claim that they fired the British armed forces' last operational .303in round of ammunition in Northern Ireland.

The markings on the sidewall of this L42A1 are common; they denote a 1971 conversion date along with the RSAF Enfield 'EFD' logo. Note the number of times the screws of the front telescope pad have been staked, suggesting that this rifle has done enough work to shake them loose only for an armourer to tighten and re-stake them. Also note the wartime Holland & Holland 'T' completion stamp as well as the manufacturer's 'KD' code on the telescope bracket, denoting Rose Brothers' manufacture (Rose Brothers used both 'JC' and 'KD' codes).

The British Army is ready to snipe again

In 1971 the MoD contract with RSAF Enfield for the conversion of No. 4 Mk 1 (T) sniping rifles to L42A1 specification was in full swing; that was the year the contract was largely fulfilled, with a great many of the L42A1 rifles bearing a 1971 conversion date on the left-hand side of the receiver. Further conversions took place in the years 1972, 1974, 1975, 1977, 1978 and 1979; and the entire decade of the 1970s saw batches of newly converted rifles being regularly dispatched by RSAF Enfield to COD Donnington central stores, each in a transit chest containing the rifle and its telescopic sight. It is thought that once the weapon entered COD Donnington central stores, each transit chest's contents were completed with the rest of the CES, which was all of the immediate equipment the rifle required to be operated and maintained by the sniper.

The final list of equipment that formed the CES was largely influenced by the Royal Marines and their use of the L42A1 in the first two to three years of its life; entirely of their design, the transit chest provided a

The L42A1 rifle is laid out with all of its CES equipment, as well as additional items such as binoculars, compass, stereoscope and scrim scarves that are drawn from stores by the sniper as supplementary issue to the rifle's CES. Note the transit-chest markings, which show that this L42A1 was used by 2nd Battalion, The Royal Green Jackets, on a brigade exercise called *Pond Jump West*, which was held annually in Canada.

L42A1 WOODWORK

Although the original specification of the L42A1 was to include all of the No. 4 Mk 1 (T) rifle's original American black-walnut wood furniture, with alterations being made to the forend and handguard during conversion to suit the new L42A1 specification, the additional machining required to widen the internal areas of the forend and handguard in preparation for the heavy, free-floating barrel and new box magazine was in many cases too much for the walnut, which at best was already 25 years old, and in some cases older still. Original walnut forends and handguards were failing during conversion and, if not at conversion, many more would fail later during their service.

The solution was found in beech wood, which was readily available and very cheap, although extremely pale for a weapon whose user heavily relied on camouflage and concealment to stay alive on the battlefield. Nevertheless, C. Moon & Co. produced new beech wood forends and handguards for the L42A1, although the buttstock was commonly the original black-walnut butt as used during the rifle's life as a No. 4 Mk 1 (T), complete with its original ash wood cheek rest, which again if replaced during or after conversion was replaced with a new-manufactured beech wood cheek rest. With respect to its wood sets, the L42A1 was quite unusual, as quite often a newly converted rifle would wear an eclectic mix of different types of wood. Some L42A1s served their entire service life with the original No. 4 Mk 1 (T) American black-walnut wood set altered at conversion, while there were others that had a beech wood forend, walnut or beech wood handguard and/or walnut buttstock fitted with an ash wood or beech wood cheek rest, which made the L42A1 look somewhat ad hoc in its appearance.

The L42A1 was hampered throughout its service by issues concerning its wood furniture. Most carried the same buttstock, this component only being changed to suit the length of pull of the individual sniper using the rifle; but buttstocks were not the problem as a great many were available from store shelves left over from the No. 4 rifles' service. The main issue lay with the specially manufactured forend and handguard, which remained susceptible to failure over the life of the L42A1: a catastrophic split in the wood was often what condemned a wooden component,

This photograph shows the rear section of a Mk 2 forend which has been retro-converted to Mk 1 specification. Note the inserts of wood, which convert the screw fixing to a tie-strap-and-rivet arrangement.

which by the mid-1980s were in short supply. This shortage became so acute that the L42A1's sister rifle – the L39A1 target rifle, which closely resembled the L42A1 and shared the same barrel – became something of a parts donor for the L42A1. The L39A1 forend was aesthetically the same, although it was in fact a Mk 2 forend whereas the L42A1 used the Mk 1, the critical difference lying mainly in how the internal area at the rear of the forend was cut. In short, the Mk 2 required modification to fit the L42A1.

With plentiful supplies of Mk 2 forends sitting in stores, the decision was made to modify these parts rather than purchasing new-manufactured forends. Many considered the problem surrounding the L42A1 and its furniture to be solved as a stop-gap solution had been found which would see the rifle into retirement, but the rifles in service would go on to consume even this new, seemingly plentiful supply of forends, which also began to run out in the mid- to late 1980s. Even so, with a trial to select a new system being imminent, there was no appetite to spend money on the L42A1, which was all but obsolete at this point. The evidence, if any were needed, that MoD funding for the L42A1 had been all but ended was seen in the pitiful state of many of the rifles when inspected prior to disposal. A great many of them had heavily worn forends showing multiple repairs to the wood, with several wearing L39A1 forends with an ad hoc conversion to make them fit.

A view from above the L42A1's forend shows the extent of the machining to accommodate the new box magazine and the heavy, free-floating barrel.

dedicated storage position for each CES item. By 1973, when the British Army commenced training its own snipers, COD Donnington central stores was in a position to begin issuing infantry battalions with eight L42A1 sniping rifles per battalion, each CES complete with transit chest, L42A1 rifle, L1A1 telescopic sight with mounting bracket, L1A1 carry case, carry case strap, leather lens covers, lens brush, lens-brush bottle, sling, cleaning kit, chamber stick, L5A1 IWS (Individual Weapon Sight) mounting bracket, 20× SRT (Scout Regiment Telescope) and user handbook.

During the initial years of the British Army's reintroduction of full-time sniper employment, the training literature governing it was largely that of the No. 4 Mk 1 (T) rifle's *Infantry Training Volume 1, Infantry Platoon Weapons Pamphlet No. 10, Sniping, 1951*, with a bridging pamphlet dated 1973 to cover the weapon-specific information until a purpose-written pamphlet could be produced. Duly appearing three years later as *Infantry Training Volume 1, Skill at Arms (Individual Training) Pamphlet No. 4, Sniping, 1976*, this would be the sole training literature for the L42A1's entire service life with the exception of a handful of amendments. Additionally, the sniper was issued a copy of the small, two-part-format *Sniper Pocket Book*, which enabled him to record ballistic data as well as being an aide-memoire specific to his role; these books are often dated 1973 or 1980.

Weapon Sight Image Intensified, L1A1

By 1973, the L42A1 rifle was fully supported by an extensive training infrastructure and was entirely compatible with Weapon Sight Image Intensified, L1A1, although when this night-vision sight entered service in 1970 it was only made available for all of the section weapons with a mounting bracket for each. This was not afforded to the L42A1 straightaway, however, with the rifle having to wait for the development of the L5A1 mounting bracket, which made the L42A1 compatible with the IWS. The night-vision sight was first issued to infantry units, with its own user handbook initially giving a short explanation as to why a mounting bracket had yet to be provided to make the device usable with the L42A1, noting that a mount for the rifle was being developed. By 1973 the development work was complete and led to the introduction of the L5A1 mounting bracket, or simply the IWS bracket, which became part of the L42A1's own CES.

The IWS was a significant advance within the sniping role, for the first time making the sniper day- and night-capable and thereby bringing a vulnerability to the enemy, who could no longer feel safe while shrouded by darkness. For a period, the IWS gave units using it a real technological edge until technology moved forward and it was countered by devices which could 'see' the infrared signature. The trade-off for this massive advantage was the weight of the IWS, which added around 2.9kg to the L42A1; moreover, the IWS was a multi-weapon sight and so there was no special consideration given as to how the L42A1-armed sniper could use it properly, good cheek weld being a constant issue. The

CARRYING THE L42A1

The means of transporting the L42A1 was limited to the robust, plywood-constructed transit chest, which was used for shipping the rifle and all its associated equipment around the world. Whether being deployed on operations, or simply on an exercise, the transit chest did its job of protecting the contents reasonably well, an indicator of this being the fact that its design was never altered. The L42A1 was also issued with a soft carry case used to sleeve the rifle once it had been removed from the transit chest. Like the rifle itself, the carry case was World War II vintage, being the Rifle No. 4 valise with a Remploy modification which included the addition of a carry strap and an additional 12.5–15cm to the No. 4 bag's length in order to accommodate the L42A1's longer barrel. The situation surrounding the soft carry case has never been clear-cut and has frustrated many users over the years, stretching back to World War II, as neither the L42A1 nor the No. 4 Mk 1 (T) could be sleeved properly in the soft carry case with the telescopic sight fitted to the rifle. World War II snipers cut the bag along the seam so a rifle fitted with the scope could be conveniently carried.

The fact is that the telescopic sight was supplied with its own No. 8 metal carry case and strap, which first appeared in 1941; later, with the introduction of the L42A1, the carry case was redesignated the Telescope Straight Sighting Cased L1A1. This may have been the catalyst for the confusion, as the scope was designed to be routinely removed from the rifle permanently fixed in its mounting bracket; when carried in the metal carry case, the mounting bracket was screwed into two brass bosses for secure transit. The carry case could then be carried with the use of a long strap, originally made of leather but later of canvas and then, as supplies became exhausted much later in the L42A1's service, of nylon.

Protests from snipers over countless years never changed this shortfall in the No. 4 bag's versatility. As early as 1973, a purpose-

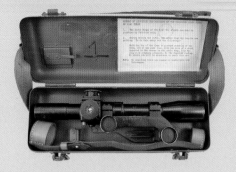

The original means of carrying the No. 32 scope was the No. 8 metal carry case, which first appeared in 1941. This example has been modified to L1A1 specification: note how the scope fixes into the carry case via the mounting bracket's thumbwheel screws. Also note the instructions glued insde the lid for the adjustment of the range scale on the elevation and windage drums.

made valise, manufactured in the same green canvas material from which the British Pattern 1958 load-carrying equipment was also made, was produced for the L42A1 in an American pattern that better suited the length of the rifle. Even so, an opportunity to improve the No. 4 bag was missed and the 1973-manufactured green carry case appears to have been a one-time-issued item that fell by the wayside; perhaps it was deemed to be too expensive to produce when No. 4 bags were in plentiful supply and could be cheaply modified by Remploy. The modified No. 4 bag is indeed the carry case that was most prolific during the L42A1's service, and it should be noted that some examples have been found to have been modified to accept the rifle with the telescopic sight fitted; some No. 4 bags have the modification while others do not, however, suggesting that this modification might have been done at unit level.

Both of the soft carry cases used in conjunction with the L42A1 are illustrated here. The No. 4 bag (above), the most widely encountered carry case, was modified by Remploy to include a carry strap and was extended to accommodate the longer barrel of the L42A1. Some No. 4 bags, including the example pictured, had an additional modification to allow the rifle to fit with the telescopic sight attached. The green carry case (below) was made in 1973 and appears to have only ever been produced once; it was the same pattern as the American Springfield case.

The L5A1 mounting bracket was used for mounting the IWS night-vision sight on the L42A1 rifle. This simple mounting bracket sat between the scope and the rifle, attaching in the same manner as the day scope's mounting bracket. Note that the contact points are not painted: this ensures that collimation is unaffected by worn paint.

This L42A1 is illustrated with the IWS night-vision sight fitted. This multi-weapon-mountable device was made available for the L42A1 between 1970 and 1973; although it was quite heavy, it broadened the sniper's role to encompass the dark hours. Very much taken for granted today, the IWS was a huge technological leap forward at the time.

IWS mounted on the L42A1 via the L5A1 mounting bracket, which made use of the two 'pads' on the left-hand side of the receiver that were primarily used for the mounting of the day scope. The job of the mounting pads was to position the telescopic sight's mounting bracket precisely before the two large thumbwheel screws the mounting bracket carried were used to secure the scope to the L42A1. The L5A1 mounting bracket was produced to mount the IWS in the same fashion and it also carried two large thumbwheel screws: these provided enough leverage for the L5A1 mounting bracket to be hand-tightened, with sprung washers behind the screws preventing them from working loose under recoil.

The IWS was a multi-weapon night-vision sight, which in turn meant its reticle had to have multi-weapon capability also. The reticle worked on the L42A1 when the rifle was zeroed at 200m with the use of L2A2 ammunition. Daytime zeroing was achieved with the heavy-duty rubber lens cover deployed: this had in its centre a small pinhole, which allowed sufficient light into the IWS without damaging its sensitive internal components.

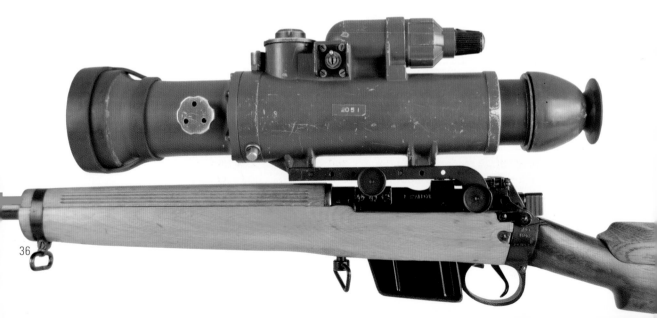

The L42A1 goes into action

The L42A1 spent a great deal of its service life in a training role connected with the Cold War, briefly interrupted by action in Dhofar and the Falklands, but crucially it saw more-or-less continuous active service in Northern Ireland as part of Operation *Banner*. The weapon was deployed effectively immediately after its introduction and was used in anger straight away during The Troubles; during an initial busy period, the L42A1 accounted for many would-be PIRA (Provisional Irish Republican Army) snipers. The Royal Marines' aggressive use of snipers during the opening years of the 1970s has been credited with forcing the PIRA to change its tactics, which as a result made the use of the security forces' own snipers in subsequent years less common, particularly as the general-issue L1A1 rifle came to be equipped with the L2A2 SUIT (Sight Unit Infantry Trilux) and image-intensified night sight, or IWS, which gave the L1A1 a day and night capability.

The PIRA terrorists were also gaining access to small arms capable of a rapid rate of fire, which could quickly outgun the L42A1 in an impromptu gun fight. Instead, the L42A1's presence was a deterrent when carried openly on patrol and its deliberate use was reserved for situations which could be tailored to the sniper, his equipment and his specialist skill set. The PIRA continued to shoot at the security forces from hidden firing points, but went on to develop a large support network around such shootings to spirit away the firearm quickly and conceal any evidence connected with the act. Such shootings were well planned and were sprung on units that had set a routine, or from positions the British Army would struggle to reach quickly and overrun, but the L42A1 was carried openly and was present in observation posts when tensions between factions on the ground erupted into violence.

This sniper is using the IWS on a well-camouflaged L42A1. Note that the sniper's face is very high; his cheek is not at all in contact with the rifle's cheek rest. This was a common problem, mainly because the IWS was a multi-weapon device that was not tailored to any particular firearm. (Courtesy of the John Coffey Collection)

Belfast, February 1978: this British soldier of the Royal Artillery is armed with the standard-issue L1A1 rifle equipped the L2A2 SUIT (Sight Unit Infantry Trilux). This was not in any way a sniping variant, but the small Trilux sight unit offered an advantage over iron sights in Northern Ireland's urban environment. The heavy-hitting 7.62mm rifle was always present during sniping operations in support of the L42A1 bolt-action rifle, particularly as the Army's adversaries had access to semi- and full-automatic weapons. (Alex Bowie/Getty Images)

One former Royal Marine who used the L42A1 in Northern Ireland recalled that while manning an observation post, he and his colleagues learned to distinguish between the sound of the British Army's SLR fire and that of the gunmen's various weapons. He recalled that in the absence of binoculars, he used the L1A1 scope for observation. One disadvantage of using the IWS was that the user experienced a few seconds' loss of

City walls, Londonderry, 1975 (opposite)

A British Army sniper pair have positioned themselves on the city walls of Londonderry overlooking the Bogside, a predominantly Catholic neighbourhood, in response to the PIRA's deployment of armed vehicle checkpoints on the streets in the local area. The sniper pair have been tasked with engaging any terrorist who presents himself as an armed target. They have made use of the city walls as they offer a commanding view of the streets below as well as solid cover from any returning fire. The spotter has found a target and is observing it with his SRT from behind a camouflage face veil he has hastily erected in the gap as he relays location, distance and corrections for a shot to the sniper. The spotter has placed his L1A1 SLR against the wall at the foot of which is his leather case for the SRT, along with the sniping rifle's L1A1 IWS night scope, which has been removed from its carry case ready for use as the light begins to fade. The sniper stands ready, supporting his L42A1 sniping rifle on a sandbag he has placed on the apex of the wall. He is marking the target the spotter has called out to him through his L1A1 telescopic sight; its leather lens caps hang free, having just been removed by the sniper as he brought the weapon to bear. He has slung the L42A1's soft carry case – which is a modified World War II-vintage No. 4 rifle bag – across his back.

vision in that eye; officially, the user was meant to use the non-shooting eye for this reason, but this was often impractical.

On one occasion, around 0100hrs, the veteran heard several pistol shots followed by the distinctive report of an SLR, coming from behind a church 430yd (393m) to his front. He was at the front of the observation post with an IWS pressed to his eye, looking for signs of movement, when the same pattern of shots was repeated, but closer. As the SLR fired a pistol-armed man ran into view, but when the sniper prepared to use his L42A1, he realized that he was still blinded in one eye by the IWS. It took only a few seconds for his vision to return, but when it did the target had moved into a doorway. The sniper put the pointer of his sight on the target's chest and took a shot, but by the time he reloaded the man has disappeared from view. Both members of the sniper pair emptied their magazines into the area around the man's previous location. Only later did it become apparent that the initial shot had been successful, hitting the target in the chest and killing him instantly.

The last hurrah

The final test for the L42A1 would come in the spring of 1982, when Argentine forces invaded the Falkland Islands on 2 April in a bid to seize them from British control. The British responded by forming a naval task force which had to transport everything required by British forces 8,000 miles south to enable them to take the fight to the Argentine forces, which by this time knew what was coming their way and used the time wisely to prepare defensive positions across a range of peaks on the islands. The Argentine positions were nestled in the rocky outcrops looking out across the slopes that fell away from their positions, which offered well-thought-out arcs of fire. The British plan of attack was originally to deliver reasonably fresh troops to each battleground by helicopter as they fought their way towards Port Stanley, but the plan had to change quickly after the sinking of the cargo ship SS *Atlantic Conveyor*, which was carrying most of the Wessex and Chinook helicopters which were vital to the plan. The only option was for the British troops to carry everything on their backs and advance to contact – 'yomping' – a practice in which British troops were well versed.

Weighing about 7.3kg, the L42A1 fitted with the IWS night scope was a heavy set-up when cradled in the arms on the long marches over challenging ground to each objective, but this combination proved deadly for the enemy. The daytime set-up would frustrate many snipers, however, as the L42A1 suffered in the wet and freezing conditions. In particular the L1A1 day scope was found wanting, with many being reported to have fogged up internally as the persistent inclement weather conditions found the weak spots in the telescopic sights' waterproofing, which was now over ten years old; the L1A1 was, after all, a refurbished World War II-vintage scope. Although it had been robust and reliable in its day, even after the overhaul it received at conversion it was severely challenged 40 years on by the conditions the South Atlantic had to offer. Among the L42A1s that suffered breakages, the greater part suffered from the failure

THE 'SF BRACKET'

In the late 1980s, during the period in which the L96A1 suffered mechanical failure, a cautious MoD – having to prepare for the possible abandonment of the L96A1 at the time – ordered a full feasibility study concerning the use of current weapon stocks as a stop-gap should the L96A1 have to be completely withdrawn from service. In 1988, the MoD commissioned 14 Maintenance Advisory Group in Woolwich, London, to carry out this study.

The evaluation looked at both the L42A1 and the L39A1, with a view to extending their service life while a new sniping rifle was found and procured. The mounting of commercial scope mounts on the L39A1 target rifle was considered, and indeed two examples were prepared, but the idea was subsequently discounted. The L42A1, which had up until very recently been the British Army's current sniping rifle, appeared to be the preferred choice of the evaluation team, who had two standard No. 32 telescopic sight mounting brackets modified to accept the 26mm tube of the L96A1's L13A1 telescopic sight. In addition, two new mounting brackets were commercially manufactured to carry the same L13A1 scope and it would be this set-up that the advisory report would recommend in the event that the L42A1 had to be utilized. As things turned out it did not, of course, but the commercially produced mounting brackets – which were beautifully made – were supplied by ITDU to the SAS for evaluation. It would be these mounting brackets that the SBS (re-designated the Special Boat Service on 24 July 1987) would later use in service, upgrading a

The device that became known as the 'SF bracket' was superbly machined from a single billet of steel then green-phosphate finished. The Royal Marines' SBS would produce these mounting brackets itself for use on its L42A1s in conjunction with both Pecar and Schmidt & Bender telescopic sights. The mounting bracket pictured was trialled by the SAS, which is why it does not have the large thumbwheel screws that got in the way of the parachute harnessing used by the SAS.

number of L42A1s to use alongside their privately procured PM rifles as well as their issued L96A1s. Over the years this mounting bracket has become known as the 'SF bracket', with claims having been made of its use on L42A1s serving with special-forces units during the 1991 Gulf War, but to date there has not been a single image, nor any personal account put forward as provenance to substantiate the claims.

of the L1A1 day scope, which led to snipers using the IWS night scope in both day and night engagements.

The Falklands War became the catalyst for change in the British armed forces and was almost certainly the event which condemned the L42A1, although the process to replace it would take several years. Since its demise there have been many fierce debates as to whether the L42A1 was really ready for retirement, with many arguing that it could have soldiered on and become an L42A2 variant with a new telescopic sight and the fitting of a synthetically bedded composite stock, which would have made the rifle comparable with the American 7.62mm M40A1 sniping rifle.

ENTER THE L96A1

The years that followed the Falklands War saw the British Army experience something of an overhaul as the conflict had exposed inadequacies across the board, from boots to small arms. It was in this post-conflict period that time was called on the L42A1 and it was added

RIFLE 7.62MM L96A1, NSN B1/1005-99-967-3405	
Calibre	7.62mm
Magazine capacity	11 rounds
Overall rifle length	46.26in (117.5cm)
Barrel length	25.5in (64.8cm)
Twist-rate	Four-groove, right-hand 1-in-14in (35.6cm)
Combat weight	14lb (6.4kg)
Iron sights	Graduated to 700m
Conversion approval date	11 March 1985
Manufactured by	Accuracy International
Scope mounted	Over bore
Contract quantity	1,112

Pictured in May 1990, this concealed sniper armed with an all-green L96A1 rifle takes aim through the L13A1 telescope. Note the red hue to the objective lens; this was a specialist coating that prevented reflection and conditioned the light passing through the device. The L13A1 would be the last British sniping scope to use the post-and-wire reticle. (Tom Stoddart/Getty Images)

to an exhaustive list of equipment which would undergo either a major upgrade or complete replacement as part of this modernization programme. Even so, it would take a further three years to select and commission a new sniping system to replace the L42A1. The year 1985 saw the MoD's selection of the PM Rifle, as it was then called, and an order was placed with AI. The PM Rifle's adoption by the MoD saw it receive a unique NATO stock number as well as its now-famous 'L96A1' nomenclature which would, after its very difficult beginnings, become synonymous with deadly long-range accuracy and begin to draw the attention of many within the global sniping community.

Function-tested L96A1s were supplied by AI with two forms of carrying system: an aluminium transit chest that housed the weapon with

all its associated equipment and a DPM (disruptive-pattern material) soft carry case with closed-cell foam padding to its sides and a zipped closure. The soft carry case was versatile, offering useful external storage space in the form of zipped and quick-release buckled pockets as well as being equipped with carry handles, a shoulder strap and a pair of backpack-type shoulder straps. AI recognized the need for a suitable carrying system when the L96A1 was not in the transit chest and addressed the long-standing issue surrounding the means of carrying the weapon when in the field by creating a soft carry case: this was not a 'drag bag' or a flimsy valise, but a capable carry case for its intended use. The soft carry case was a major improvement on what was previously issued with the L42A1, so much so that it was used by snipers through the L96A1's entire service life, much length of service being the true litmus test of any piece of military kit.

The L96A1 came with a comprehensive set of CES items; the group of accessories were well thought out by people who were not from a military background but instead came from the highest levels of civilian competitive target shooting. This involvement of individuals from the competitive-shooting world was set to advance sniping within Britain's military far beyond what was thought possible at the time. Furthermore, it is an interesting fact that yet again, as with the genesis of the L42A1, the L96A1 was born through civilian competitive shooting, with the military being indebted to the civilian shooting community for its advances in rifle design and barrel technology, embodied in the sniping rifles that made it into service after the British Army reintroduced sniping. The design of the L96A1 and the maintenance and cleaning tools that came with it revolutionized the British sniper's custodial responsibilities for his rifle, providing an unprecedented level of access as well as a completely overhauled cleaning regime. For the first time, the cleaning regime involved use of a bore guide, cleaning rod and phosphor-bronze bore brush in combination with carbon- and copper-removal agents, in contrast to the cleaning regime of the L42A1, which was simply cleaned with a standard pull-through and flannelette. The very highest standards of civilian cleaning and maintenance were now extended to the military sniping rifle, with thorough practices regarding post-firing cleaning being observed as standard practice.

The action/telescope dust cover was produced and issued as a standard CES item; little did anyone realize what an important item it would prove to be, given the L96A1's extensive combat use in desert conditions during Operation *Desert Storm*. The first variant, pictured here, was produced in a DPM camouflage material; a second variant was produced in plain green and with slightly more generous proportions.

In 1986, when the L96A1 was first issued, the CES items list included the following: L96A1 rifle, three magazines, sling, L13A1 sight complete in mounting bracket, cleaning rod (long), cleaning rod (short), cleaning kit, brass jag, phosphor-bronze bore brush, 2.5mm Allen key, 4mm Allen key, 5mm Allen key, 35mm-long screwdriver, rigid carry case, soft carry case, telescope/action dust cover, muzzle cap and protective caps for the L13A1 sight.

For the first four years, the training literature was *Infantry Training Volume 1, Skill at Arms (Individual Training) Pamphlet No. 4, Sniping, 1976* as used with the L42A1, and as with the introduction of the L42A1 the previous training pamphlet continued along with a bridging pamphlet which covered weapon-specific information. In the case of the L96A1 this was *Infantry Training Volume 1, Skill at Arms (Individual Training) Supplement to Pamphlet No. 4, Sniping, 1986* until 1990, when the first purpose-written pamphlet for the L96A1 emerged with the same title. In 1996 an amended version of the same pamphlet was issued, which would see the L96A1 through to the end of its service life. The *Sniper Pocket Book* also continued in the same two-part format as that issued to the L42A1 sniper; it continued to be housed in the transit chest with *Rifle, Sniper, 7.62mm, L96A1 Operating Information*, which was essentially the user handbook for the sniper's own reference.

The L96A1 tested in combat

In the early years, the L96A1's service life would be much like that of the L42A1, with a presence in Northern Ireland as well as routine Cold War training until that era came to an end with the dissolution of the Soviet Union in 1991. The opportunity to raise the profile of the L96A1 also came in early 1991, during Operation *Desert Storm*, which was the operational name for the combat phase (January–February) of the Gulf War. In 1941, 50 years earlier, the British Army's previous attempt to deploy snipers to a desert theatre of operations had involved the No. 4 Mk 1 (T) rifle equipped with the No. 32 Mk 1 telescopic sight. On that

British snipers during Operation *Desert Storm*, 1991 (opposite)

British forces have pushed deep into Kuwait to engage with Iraqi forces. A British sniper pair are operating on the forward edge of their battlegroup to collect intelligence and to look for priority targets of opportunity. US Air Force A-10A Thunderbolt II 'tank-buster' aircraft have already swept through, leaving a number of Iraqi vehicles burning. As the Iraqi forces withdrew, they set fire to the oilfields out in the desert; the thick black smoke can be seen for miles. The sniper pair have located a T-72 main battle tank of the Iraqi Republican Guard; the Soviet-built tank is stranded and on its own, having probably broken down. The tank crew are still manning the vehicle, either waiting for help to arrive or preparing to abandon it. The sniper pair observe the target, weighing up the risks of opening fire on a tank which – although immobile – can still bring a huge amount of firepower to bear.

This L96A1 has been laid out with all of its CES equipment. Note the sticks on the DPM rifle bag; these were made by the sniper and offered a steady platform from which to shoot and to observe.

occasion the weapon, or rather its primitive scope, proved completely inadequate in the North African desert environment, being plagued by failure issues due to heat, dust and sand which subsequently ended any ideas the British may have had regarding desert sniping for the rest of World War II. British snipers armed with the L96A1 during Operation *Desert Storm* had an experience entirely different from that of their World

War II predecessors: they enjoyed good 'hunting' with a weapon that was very capable in this, the most inhospitable of environments that was notorious for breaking equipment.

Fortuitously, the well-thought-out CES of each L96A1 also included three items that were not desert-specific, but which were to aid the weapon's daily use immensely in this punishing environment: an action/telescope dust cover and a plastic muzzle cap were extremely effective in keeping dust and sand away from the telescope/receiver and from entering the barrel when the weapon was not in use, while the third item – the transparent lens cover for the L13A1 telescopic sight – could remain on the scope during use if the wind was kicking up dust and dirt, thereby saving the scope's lenses and their protective films from the destructive desert environment. The lenses and their protective films were vital in conditioning the light being transmitted through the optic. Although they suffered the effects of the abrasive dust and sand, the lens covers were a very cheap and effective – albeit sacrificial – way of preserving the scope's lenses from damage. All in all, the L13A1 telescopic sight was extremely robust and set the standard for future British sniping optics.

Snipers armed with the L96A1/L13A1 combination are reported to have done a great deal of deadly work during Operation *Desert Storm*, particularly while they stalked the flanks of Highway 80, otherwise known as the 'Highway of Death', which became an escape route for Iraqi forces fleeing from Kuwait. Many Iraqi combatants who met their end on the 'Highway of Death' did so at the hands of British snipers who remained concealed far out in the desert wastelands that bordered both sides of the giant highway, which extended all the way back to Iraq.

These students of the Royal Marines are using the SRT, or 'Antique Brass', as late as 1994. They are sitting on an observation stand and are looking for small items of kit secreted in the landscape ahead of them. Note that they are using steel trip-flare pickets to support their telescopes. (Courtesy of Chris Harrison)

COMMON WEAPON SIGHT, L8A2

Modern warfare is a 24-hour business for all involved, including snipers. The L96A1 was able to operate day and night with the L8A2 CWS (Common Weapon Sight) night scope, and the L13A1 day scope which was permanently held in its detachable mount. Like the mounting brackets of the L1A1 day scope and the IWS mounting bracket of the L42A1, both the CWS and the L13A1 scope mounting brackets had two large thumbwheel screws for tightening the mounting brackets once located on the dovetailed receiver. The CWS night scope was made available for the L96A1; at this point it was the only means of night vision, being made weapon-capable via its own L14A1 mounting bracket, which became part of the L96A1's own CES equipment in 1992. As with its predecessor, the CWS reticle offered multi-weapon capability, and for the L96A1 worked specifically with L2A2 ammunition. In order to use the CWS, the L13A1 day scope had to be removed from the L96A1 so that the CWS could attach via the L14A1 mount, which utilized the dovetail on the rifle's receiver in the same way that the L13A1's mount attached.

As with the L42A1's IWS night scope, the CWS, being intended for multiple weapons, brought with it issues that the sniper simply had to put up with, such as the scope's high position on the weapon, which generated cheek-weld issues. Even so, the relatively new CWS represented a huge leap forward from the IWS, being just over one-third of the weight and a fraction of the size of its predecessor, and offering much-improved image quality with which the sniper was expected to achieve kills at a maximum distance of 600m. The CWS was still susceptible to light damage, however, if the device was switched on and exposed to daylight with its rubber lens cover removed. For use in urban environments such as Northern Ireland, where at night the street lighting could be as damaging as daylight, the CWS was issued with a dense black filter lens.

The L8A2 CWS night scope is shown here mounted on the L96A1. Like its forebear, the scope's high position on the rifle presented the sniper with cheek-weld issues. The problem was not helped by the fact that two mounting brackets had to be used to mount the scope on the L96A1. The CWS has its own mount fixed to its underside; this then fitted in turn to the L14A1 mount that attached to the receiver of the L96A1.

'Creeping sniper excellence'

The mid-1990s saw the L96A1 approaching a decade of service, during which time the snipers who used it had long realized that its 'reach' was far greater than that which had been taught as part of British sniper doctrine since 1973, which was 'deadly fire' out to 600m and 'harassing fire' out to 800m. Operation *Desert Storm* saw British snipers routinely delivering 'deadly fire' out to 800m and beyond; this brought about an

officially recognized change to *Pamphlet No. 4*, increasing the maximum 'deadly fire' distance to 900m, while the 'harassing fire' distance was increased to 1,100m.

Even after a decade of service, the accuracy of the L96A1 was still prompting change within sniper platoons across the British Army, so much so that sniper pairs in some units were becoming frustrated by the limited capability of the optics being made available to the spotter, who was not able to locate and direct the sniper on to targets out to the maximum distances at which the sniper could realistically engage. Even as late as the mid-1990s, some units were still using the 20× SRT – or 'Antique Brass', as it was dubbed due to that style of telescope having notched up around 100 years of service at this point – while others used the 15–60× Swift Telescope. Although the Swift Telescope had the power the spotter so desperately needed as well as a generally good service record, having been used reliably in other areas of the military, it failed disastrously with snipers operating in the desert. This was because its focus and magnification controls acted as an entry point for the fine powdery dust which slowly filled the internal compartments, rendering the telescope useless.

The L96A1's long-range accuracy was the catalyst for snipers and their spotters to actively seek out the ideal optic for the job. Although the SRT had by 1990 been officially superseded by the American M49 Spotting Scope (also known as the M49 Observation Telescope) and its M15 tripod, modified by United Scientific Instruments Ltd of Kenilworth, Warwickshire for British service with the addition of an integral sunshade, the M49 offered just 20× magnification, which was inadequate for the maximum distances at which the L96A1 could engage.

There was in this period of the 1990s a wide selection of good-quality spotting telescopes being made available on the civilian market,

The Swift (left) and M49 (right) telescopes were both inadequate, albeit for different reasons. Although it offered a huge 60× magnification, the Swift was not robust enough for sniper service. While the M49 Spotting Scope was a battle-proven design, it did not offer enough power to match the ability of the L96A1, its magnification being just 20×, which led to the private purchase of various types of spotter telescopes from the civilian market.

intended for wildlife enthusiasts. Many units were quick to capitalize on this selection by making private purchases of their own spotter optics from the commercial market, in which there was a wide choice from manufacturers such as Greenkat, Opticron and Kowa. All of these spotting telescopes, although excellent, varied in some way from one another, however, whether in terms of the quality of the lenses or the power of magnification they offered; even so, they all – in stark contrast to the SRT and M49 – allowed the spotter to identify targets clearly out to 1,000m and beyond. This unauthorized use of an eclectic mix of privately purchased spotting telescopes led to a practice known as 'Creeping Sniper Excellence', a term used for the increasing variety of practices that began to evolve unsanctioned outside the strictures of *Pamphlet No. 4*, leading to snipers of individual units adopting equipment and practices that differed from other units' methods and official British sniping doctrine.

Mid-life upgrade and access to cutting-edge optics

In the wake of the 1991 Gulf War, the L96A1 was seen by many as a proven success, should proof have been needed to win around the staunch few who still favoured the Parker-Hale M85. The L96A1 had already caught the eye of other potential users around the world – notably the Swedes, who would play a significant role in bringing the next generation of AI rifle to the fore. The Swedes asked AI to design them a rifle that was based on the L96A1 and capable of operating faultlessly in sub-zero conditions. This was key to the emergence of the AW rifle, which the British MoD would go on to adopt exclusively for special-forces units. The 1990s would see AI continue to develop the AW platform while the L96A1 continued to serve into the 21st century. Shortly after the British adoption in the late 1990s of the AW rifle, or L118A1 as it was designated, the L96A1 received an upgraded telescopic sight, the same 3–12×50mm Schmidt & Bender PM scope – designated the L17A1 – which was standard to the L118A1; this telescopic sight formed the main part of the L96 A1 rifle's midlife upgrade.

The midlife upgrade of the L96A1 saw it receive the 3–12×50mm L17A1 telescopic sight, which heralded many more years of service. With this new and more powerful optic, the L96A1 was routinely able to deliver lethal fire at 900m and beyond.

Nearly 20 years after the L96A1 was first adopted, fitting the new L17A1 telescopic sight to the weapon was an upgrade which offered a chance to bring out the best of the rifle's potential. The L17A1 used the P4 mildot reticle developed by the US Marine Corps, the purpose of which was to assist the sniper in ranging the target as well as providing data to

The advent of the L17A1 telescopic sight gave the L96A1 access to cutting-edge optics. This photograph depicts the rifle fitted with the later-specification forend block, which not only carries the bipod but also accommodates a Picatinny siderail to enable the mounting of a STIC scope.

be used for holding off for wind, bullet drop and moving targets. When corrections were dialled into the scope, it was now graduated in milliradian 0.1 fine adjustment tactile and audible clicks. The L17A1 also came with a sunshade and a honeycomb Killflash filter, intended to eliminate any light glinting off the objective lens. This was a recurrent issue given the L96A1's now seemingly eternal desert presence, where bright sunshine catching the objective lens would betray a sniper's position from many miles away; a problem that was ever present while the sun was out but which was particularly hazardous when the L96A1 'jumped' on recoil. Snipers equipped with the L96A1 fitted with the L13A1 telescopic sight during the 1991 Gulf War did not have the luxury of a purpose-made Killflash filter and would instead improvise with a piece of scrim netting taped over the objective lens, which was equally as effective.

The L17A1 telescopic sight's larger dimensions meant that the L96A1 had to lose its back-up sights, primarily because the rear sight would no longer fit under the scope. That said, the provision of back-up sights was by this time becoming a thing of the past, possibly because there is little evidence that they had ever been used in a combat situation after 1945.

Use of the L17A1 in conjunction with the L96A1 rifle was significant and underlined how advanced the L96A1 was when it first entered service. The upgrade heralded many more years of service for the rifle, coming at a point in its service life at which its predecessor, the L42A1, had been withdrawn from service in a very tired state. The L17A1 telescopic sight also heralded further revision of training *Pamphlet No. 4* due to its increased variable power of magnification; it brought about more challenging observation testing on the sniper course for the students attending.

Upgrading the L96A1 with the L17A1 telescope meant the rifle could be used with the most cutting-edge night-vision devices which, after the Iraq War began in March 2003, were often purchased by the MoD as Key Operational Equipment. During the Iraq War, British special-forces units were the first to employ advanced image intensifiers and thermal-imaging devices. The L17A1 was capable of operating with the SIMRAD, which was a 'piggyback' night-vision device that turned what was a day scope into a fully functioning night scope. The device could be mounted on the day scope via a small mounting bracket located atop the L17A1's own front mount ring; it slid on to the mounting bracket and was fixed in place via a locking lever. The SIMRAD collected the available light through a 100mm-diameter lens that sat above the L17A1 and offered just 1× magnification, as the day scope utilized its own 3–12× magnification as well as its own reticle. The sniper was now effectively looking through the SIMRAD via a prism, which meant his point of aim was altered by 120mm, something he had to be aware of when selecting his shot placement on his chosen target.

Another device that was initially used exclusively by British special-forces units was the STIC (Sniper Thermal Image Capability) scope, which again worked in conjunction with the L17A1 day scope by being mounted directly in front of the objective lens. The sniper pair were issued with two STIC scopes – one for the weapon and a second, handheld device for the spotter – so the pair could both view the target in the same way. The STIC was mounted offset in conjunction with the use of a Picatinny siderail, so as to allow the STIC scope to be mounted on the L96A1. The rifle's forend block, which carried the bipod, was redesigned to accommodate not only the bipod but also a detachable Picatinny siderail specifically to enable the mounting of the STIC.

British snipers of 1st Battalion, The Irish Guards are pictured in Basra, Iraq, in April 2003. The pair are armed with L96A1 sniping rifles heavily clad in sniper tape. The rifles have received the mid-life upgrade and are pictured without battle sights and fitted with the L17A1 telescope. The upgraded weapon facilitated the development of the sniper's role; these snipers are providing overwatch for troops on the ground, in this case personnel of the Royal Engineers extinguishing oil-well fires. (Giles Penfound/MOD/Getty Images)

The beginning of the end for the L96A1

The L96A1 received its upgrade in time for its epic return to the desert in 2002 during the war in Afghanistan (2002–14) as part of Operation *Herrick*. In the following year it would also find itself in another desert in another country as part of Operation *Telic*, the codename for the Iraq War (2003–11). The L96A1 was unprecedented as a sniper system and would be active through a period of continuous combat extending over 13 years amid dust, sand and searing heat. Nevertheless, in 2008 the L96A1 slowly began to be withdrawn from service over a four-year period after the British Army committed to the biggest modernization of its sniper equipment in history.

The Taliban fighters in Afghanistan had by 2008 become skilled at fighting just outside the effective range of the British Army forces, with many engagements taking place well beyond the 300m effective combat range of the 5.56mm L85A2 assault rifle. This frustrated the troops on the ground, who were expending huge amounts of small-arms ammunition in these firefights – quite often against just a handful of fighters – with much of it proving to be ineffective. Unfortunately, the trusty L96A1 became increasingly ineffective against the Taliban fighters, who tailored their tactics to counter those employed by their British Army opponents.

In previous years, British special-forces units – including SFSG, which at the time was 1st Battalion, The Parachute Regiment – used not only advanced night-vision equipment but also the AW rifle in a much larger calibre. The AW rifle was produced to chamber the .338in Lapua Super Magnum cartridge, which proved to be devastatingly accurate at distances much greater than those achievable with the L96A1. Over shorter distances, while the sniper using the 7.62mm cartridge had to consider the effects of a breeze in order to deliver his ammunition accurately on a target which might offer only a single brief opportunity, the bigger and more powerful .338in cartridge would power through any such conditions with a much better chance of a first-round hit delivering an unsurvivable wound.

British special-forces units had demonstrated how the 'Engagement Envelope' could be increased with the use of the AW rifle; this not only paved the way for a historic overhaul of sniping equipment in 2008, but also the L96A1's withdrawal from service. The withdrawal was complete by 2012, by which time the L96A1 was looking a rather tired weapon – although, it has to be said, still very capable. At this point, all L96A1s were in stores and faced an unknown future. Various proposals were made regarding their future use: these included a complete refurbishment and reissue to the British Army as a lighter short- to mid-range sniping rifle, as well as gifting them to the Afghan National Army prior to the British Army's planned withdrawal from Afghanistan in 2014. None of these proposals would come to fruition, however, as in late 2014 and early 2015 the entire 'Green Fleet', as the L96A1 was collectively dubbed, was destroyed and the collection of parts disposed of in the North Sea, presumably to prevent a single piece becoming a highly collectable war trophy of sorts. After all, the L96A1 had completed nearly 30 years of

THE L96A1 ALMOST FOUGHT ON

The trade-off for the L115A3 rifle's long-range capability was the weapon's weight (6.9kg) and length (1.23m), which made it a difficult weapon to wield in close combat. The L96A1, which had this versatility, was rapidly disappearing and leaving in its place a vacuum, with snipers crying out for a weapon which was lighter and easier to bring to bear on targets within a 300m range, this often being the distance within which an engagement or ambush would be triggered against British forces. AI, or more accurately Dave Walls, heard this complaint directly from snipers visiting the company's manufacturing facility in Portsmouth, and responded by modifying an L96A1 rifle to become a weapon which, on first inspection, resembled the AW rifle. The rifle was given a folding buttstock and a 20in (50.8cm) barrel which was completed with the same double-chamber muzzle brake as that of the L115A3. In short, the modified L96A1 was turned into a highly mobile short- to mid-range weapon capable of extreme accuracy; furthermore, the 'Green Fleet' was held in stores, ready to be converted.

The new weapon was presented to the MoD, which very quickly dismissed it out of hand. Instead, infantry units received the American Armalite Rifle platform in 7.62×51mm NATO calibre, manufactured by LMT (Lewis Machine & Tool Company) of Eldridge, Iowa. Designated the L129A1 Sharpshooter, the new weapon was supplied with a large Trijicon ACOG (Advanced Combat Optical Gunsight) sight; it was not specifically issued to snipers, but instead to members of a rifle section trained as sharpshooters, whose role was to be the immediate response to short- to mid-range engagements.

The L129A1 was quickly adopted by the sniper pair as the SSW (Sniper Support Weapon) and fitted with the L17A1 telescopic sight taken from the retired L96A1s. A major criticism of the L129A1 is its lack of forward assist – ordinarily a standard feature on the Armalite Rifle platform – which in turn has caused the weapon to experience the very problems the forward assist was designed to overcome; but as the SSW it has proven to be very accurate out to 800m, allowing the spotter to join the fight when necessary and support the sniper with accurate suppressing fire.

At the time of writing, the L115A3 is set to remain as the British Army's principal sniping system for at least another decade. When change comes, its receiver will be refurbished to that of the AX ('A' denotes AI, and 'X' denotes the inner scoring ring on a target) L115A4 specification, as was the L115A3's receiver from both the L115A1 and L115A2 specifications. AI has already long ceased producing the AW rifle for the civilian market and the weapon lives on in manufacture purely as a military-supplied rifle, but the L115A4 from the AX generation of weapons is already slowly replacing the AWSM and will in time completely supersede the AW family of rifles.

In 2008, the British sniper pair armed with the L115A3 remained incomplete, but in 2009 was set to become a powerful two-man cell with the introduction of the L129A1 Sharpshooter rifle. In the hands of the section sharpshooter, the weapon was day- and night-capable with the use of MUNS (Magnum Universal Night Sight), an inline night-vision telescope which sat in front of the ACOG. Spotters adopted the L129A1 as the SSW and replaced the ACOG

service and had seen significant combat use in various conflicts over that time, accounting for a great many enemy lives.

A sniping rifle that could deliver fiercely accurate and deadly fire at relatively short ranges, as well as punishingly effective and harassing fire at double the maximum range of the L96A1, had been found and was set to create havoc among Taliban fighters, who had become very bold with their tactic of taking on British forces from a carefully gauged distance. The .338in AWSM rifle began its British Army career in the mid-1990s in the L115A1 specification. In the early 2000s it received several improvements of which Dave Caig's folding stock was the principal feature, resulting in the L115A2 variant.

THE L115A3 ENTERS SERVICE

The decision was taken in 2007 to overhaul the British Army's sniping capability completely, by replacing the L96A1 across the entire field army with a new .338-calibre L115A3 Long Range Rifle variant. The

British sniper pairs adopted the L129A1 in its Sharpshooter set-up as the SSW, replacing the ACOG sight with the L17A1. As the SSW the L129A1 was often used alongside the L115A3 with a suppressor fitted. (Image by Stuart Hill; © Crown copyright 2016)

with the 3–12×50 L17A1 telescopic sight previously used with the L96A1. This practice allowed SIMRAD to be used in place of MUNS and it also gave the sniper a day- and night-capable back-up scope; in the event that his L24A1 telescopic sight malfunctioned or became battle-damaged, the sniper could simply mount the L17A1 on the L115A3 and the spotter would then rely on his battle sights, which came as standard on the L129A1.

In addition to this, the spotter used a SureFire suppressor in conjunction with the SSW for tactical uniformity with the sniper's L115A3, which was predominantly used with its short tactical suppressor fitted. The sniper's suppressor assisted with reducing the L115A3's recoil, but more importantly – and particularly when the rifle was used at long range – the suppressor concealed the sniper pair's position. At extreme long range the enemy would be unable to work out where the shot came from, as it would be unlikely that they would even hear the report of the weapon; their first realization that they were in trouble would be the crack of the round as it streaked through their position, and possibly one of their number. The 'thump' – the weapon's report, which would ordinarily follow – would be inaudible, thus denying the enemy the opportunity to work out the direction of the shot and gauge the distance. At night the suppressor would also conceal the L115A3's muzzle flash, so it made complete sense for the spotter also to make every effort to conceal any shot he might be required to take, causing fear and confusion among the enemy and maintaining the psychological suspense the sniper pair brought to the battlefield.

decision was confirmed with an MoD order placed with AI for an initial 582 L115A3s with delivery scheduled for 2008. The SSIP modernization and improvement of the British Army's sniping capability delivered a specialist weapon to British units serving in Afghanistan in 2008. The L115A3 was capable of extreme long-range precision in any weather and at any time of the day and was to some degree built with the vast open Afghan plains in mind. The British Army fully intended to make the most of the L115A3's capabilities and so the new rifle was fielded with a suite of equipment to assist both the sniper and the spotter in their delivery of fire. Designated the L24A1, the 5–25× telescopic sight is a Schmidt & Bender PM Mk II with a 56mm-diameter objective lens. The reticle retained the same P4 mildot reticle with bracketing ranging stadia lines used in the L17A1. The elevation drum still adjusted in milliradians; the L24A1 is specifically a big-calibre scope, with the elevation drum (marketed by Schmidt & Bender as 'Dual Turn') rotating just twice. Parallax adjustment was still present, with the addition of a reticle which, at the discretion of the sniper, could be illuminated via its own control.

RIFLE .338 LAPUA AWSM L115A3, NSN 1005-99-372-3045	
Calibre	.338in
Magazine capacity	Five rounds single stack
Overall rifle length	1,230mm
Barrel length	27in (68.6cm)
Twist-rate	Right-hand 1-in-11in (27.9cm)
Combat weight	6.9kg
Iron sights	No
Conversion approval date	October 2007
Manufactured by	Accuracy International
Scope mounted	Over bore
Contract quantity	582

Salisbury Plain, England, March 2008: a British sniper clad in a fully camouflaged concealment vest lies behind an extremely new-looking L115A3 rifle and takes aim through the L24A1 telescope. This .338in rifle began several years earlier specifically as the Long Range Rifle in an A1 variant, but as snipers became more in demand during Operation *Herrick* in Afghanistan, the large calibre and the reach it provided made the L115A3 the principal sniping system of the British Army. (In Pictures Ltd./Corbis via Getty Images)

The L24A1 telescopic sight ended the use of BDC as it had been recognized for the previous 20 years: distance referencing numbers, which had become commonplace on the elevation drum, were now omitted. Snipers now used ASATS (Advanced Small Arms Targeting System), computer software containing ballistic data sheets for temperate, desert and arctic environments. The software measures the individual L115A3's muzzle velocity; the sniper then selects the muzzle-velocity figure closest to that of his own L115A3 in the software, which contains ballistic data charts matching the 252-grain bullet in each of the aforementioned climate zones, and then selects the ballistic data that best suits the operational conditions.

It is hard to tell whether this outcome is intentional or not, but the L115A3 is now essentially a 252-grain specialist weapon with a great deal of ballistic data now tailored to the weapon and its ammunition. There are also some physical features of the L115A3 that restrict it to the use of this ammunition, however, such as the magazine, which is designed to seat this specific length of cartridge. Furthermore, the L115A3's fluted barrel, 27in (68.6cm) in length, is manufactured with a twist-rate for this round. The fluted barrel is also specific to British Army specification as AI does not offer this barrel to any other customer due to accuracy inconsistencies during development. The inconsistencies came directly as a result of the fluting, which for operational reasons the British Army continued to specify, deeming it to be a reasonable trade-off against the reduced weight and convection cooling the fluting brings, although many argue that these benefits are negligible.

SIMRAD and STIC

The L24A1 telescopic sight's mounting bracket also accommodated the use of the KN 203D SIMRAD image intensifier, which was also standard issue as part of the SSIP. The device was, however, still dependent upon enough available light being emitted from the stars and/or moon to be intensified for the device to be of any use; this could not be guaranteed, of course, and on the blackest of nights the device was essentially rendered useless for the purposes of sniping, which did not aid the 24-hour vocation of the new sniping system. After all, the purpose of the SSIP was to deliver a weapon which was truly combat-ready in all weathers and around the clock. With this in mind, the STIC scope was also made available to the sniper for those occasions when night-time conditions were poor and unsuitable for the KN 203D SIMRAD.

Manufactured by Qioptiq Ltd of St Asaph, Denbighshire, and marketed as the SVIPIR-2, or Sniper Viper Sight Mk 2, the STIC scope is like a great deal of equipment the British field army eventually receives in that it had already been used to destruction during considerable service with special-forces units. It was now available to unit snipers not only for use on occasions when there was insufficient light for the KN 203D SIMRAD, but also in daylight when weather conditions made the use of the conventional day scope difficult. This was possible due to the STIC reading thermal signature rather than being dependent upon light being transmitted through the device.

The STIC is mounted on the L115A3 in line with the L24A1 day scope, in the same way the L24A1 was mounted on the L96A1 rifle, although the Picatinny siderail has been altered to accommodate the L24A1's bigger (56mm-diameter) objective lens. The two devices were then connected via a light-cancelling sheath. As with SIMRAD, the L24A1 day scope continued to be used as normal, but the sniper's view of the world was now a thermal one. The routine deployment of the STIC in Afghanistan led to problems, however, as it was used in several 'blue on blue' engagements; this drew considerable criticism of its function, because allowing the sniper to see his target only as a thermal

The KN 203D SIMRAD image intensifier was the model rolled out across the field army as part of the SSIP. The night-vision device revolutionized sniping through the dark hours as the sniper could continue to use his day scope in the normal way, which meant that precise corrections for a first-round hit could be dialled into the day scope as would be done in daylight. Note how the KN 203D SIMRAD slides on to the large mount on the day scope's mounting bracket and locks with two locking levers.

image made positive identification impossible beyond 300–400m, even though the device can reveal a man out to 1,000m. The STIC is also handicapped quite severely once multiple rounds have been fired: being a thermal-imaging device, it does not operate well when the sniper looks directly along the top of a hot barrel, as this creates a mirage effect that deforms the target picture. This problem could have been overcome with a simple accessory previously issued to special-forces units with the L118A1 rifle – an elasticated mirage band that ran the length of the barrel and physically blocked the heat from radiating up in front of the telescope. The mirage band was not the only potentially useful item to be absent from the L115A3's CES, however.

The L115A3 was also the first sniping rifle issued to the British Army to be made available without back-up sights to its L24A1 telescope. The reasoning behind this omission is unclear, but the modern chain of supply is so impressive that a defective optic can be replaced within a 24-hour period – a factor which has contributed to this once-standard feature now being a thing of the past.

The Sniper Viper Sight Mk 2 – or STIC as it is officially titled – offers snipers an alternative way of seeing in the dark, or in daylight hours through bad weather; regardless of the time of day, the STIC can be used to locate the enemy even when he is particularly well-hidden. This photograph illustrates how the STIC is mounted on the Picatinny siderail and connects with the day scope via a light-cancelling sheath. Like the KN 203D SIMRAD device, the STIC allows the day scope to be used in the normal way.

SSIP equipment

To deliver the sniper pair's ammunition on target every time and with the consideration that much of it would be delivered at long range, new tools to assist the pair were introduced. The spotter received a new spotting telescope, which was powerful enough to work effectively alongside the rifle, whether it was the L96A1 prior to its withdrawal or the heavier-calibre L115A3; a successful partnership, which was never quite fulfilled previously, had been achieved. Entering service in 2008, the new officially issued spotting telescope was the 12–40× Leupold Mk 4, fitted with the same P4 mildot reticle as used in the L24A1 telescopic sight, so both sniper and spotter have exactly the same sight picture of the target. The Leupold Mk 4 spotting telescope has a 60mm-diameter objective lens and comes with a honeycomb Killflash filter, Cullman tripod and soft carry case.

To assist the spotter further with his task of calling the shot, especially when the shot could be conducted at ranges greater than 1,500m, a Kestrel 3000 pocket weather meter was also made available. Used in conjunction with the spotting telescope, the Kestrel 3000 enables the spotter to measure acute changes in wind strength and humidity – vital information which the sniper requires when dialling in to his telescopic sight the corrections required for the bullet's path to a target which may be a considerable distance away.

In terrain such as that encountered in Afghanistan, the shot may be down – or up, for that matter – a long slope, or even a very steep angle. To address this, a simple drop-mounted device called a cosine indicator was fitted to the receiver's Picatinny siderail, the small

November 2012, Helmand, Afghanistan: a British sniper is pictured armed with an L115A3 rifle equipped with an L24A1 telescope. Note the SIMRAD night-vision mount, which is integral to the scope mount itself. (Jerome Starkey/Moment/Getty Images)

The Leupold Mk 4 spotting telescope was designated the L1A1 for British service. The telescope is pictured on its Cullman tripod with its honeycomb Killflash filter fitted. The reticle in the L1A1 is identical to the reticle the sniper has in the L24A1 telescopic sight, so both the spotter and sniper can view a target in the same way.

device sitting on the left side of the receiver and conveniently positioned so it can be read by the sniper when in a firing position. (The British version of this device reads cosine whereas the American version is in degrees.) Regardless of the straight line-of-sight distance, shooting uphill or downhill reduces the corrections that would normally apply for the same distance along flat ground. To calculate the corrections for an angled shot measured by cosine a simple mathematical formula is used. The weapon is aimed at the target and the cosine measurement from the device is noted. This measurement figure is then multiplied by the line-of-sight distance measurement figure, the resulting number being a distance figure for which the sniper's sight has corrections dialled in.

This spotter is using the Kestrel 3000 pocket weather meter in conjunction with the L1A1 Mk 4 spotting telescope while he observes the path the bullet will take to the target. He uses both devices to read the conditions and relays to the sniper any changes he is required to make to the telescope's corrections in order for their ammunition to strike first time. (Image by Stuart A Hill AMS; © Crown copyright 2017)

A close-up of the cosine indicator. This robust device is simplicity itself, yet it provides reliable critical information to aid the sniper when he has to calculate an angled shot. Note that the readings on the device are the same either side of zero for uphill or downhill readings.

The L115A3 is a long-range engagement weapon; when it was used in the wide-open spaces of Afghanistan, British snipers actively looked for targets which could make the most of the rifle's long-range capability and would be psychologically damaging to the enemy. In order for these distant targets to be ranged accurately, the sniper pair also received a new, less bulky, electronic pocket laser rangefinder, the Vectronix PLRF 15c, which was capable of a number of tasks. First, the 'c' in the designation denotes 'compass'; as well as showing the compass bearing, the PLRF 15c is capable of measuring the distance from the device out to a maximum of 3,000m with an accuracy of ±2m. The PLRF 15c can range multiple targets, which is very useful when

Another modern wonder made available through the SSIP. The Vectronix PLRF 15c pocket laser rangefinder is the perfect partner to the L115A3 rifle, providing accurate measurement to target at extreme distances. The device is accurate over short to mid-ranges when handheld, but for distant objects it can be used with a tripod as a steady platform for precise readings.

The Eberlestock load-carrying system is pictured here broken down into its individual components. The large scabbard and hood conceal the L115A3 rifle with its buttstock folded. To deceive the eye further, the set-up has an integrated medium-size backpack.

plotting the route of a stalk or for coordinating the activities of several snipers to deliver simultaneous fire on multiple targets such as an enemy patrol.

The L115A3 very quickly delivered the desired effect on an enemy that had become overconfident in its actions against British forces in Helmand Province, so much so that snipers became targets of the highest priority for the Taliban. British Army patrols were scrutinized by 'Dickers' (civilian spotters), who reported the movements of troops and what equipment they were carrying; a particular piece of kit they were always on the lookout for

The L115A3 is laid out with all of its CES items and associated equipment. Note the Eberlestock load-carrying system packed in its own backpack.

was the 'long gun' (sniping rifle) and when such a weapon was spotted, considerable efforts would be made to eliminate the sniper in that patrol. To combat this, snipers would fold the buttstock of the sniping rifle and cradle it like it was an L85A2 assault rifle, which fooled the Dickers for a while until they realized that the L115A3 weapon had a folding stock. Members of The Rifles and The Parachute Regiment report that patrolling with a sniping rifle at this point became too dangerous and relied on the sniping rifle being delivered to them by vehicle or helicopter once they reached their objective; this solved the problem in part, but it left the patrol without this hugely effective asset en route. The solution came in the form of the Eberlestock load-carrying system, which carried the sniping rifle vertically with the buttstock folded in a scabbard and also had an integrated backpack. The result was a load-carrying system that looked like a regular military backpack; it was successful in its deception, although today the cat is almost certainly out of the bag as several companies now manufacture their own take on this system and market it worldwide.

IMPACT
Trial and error, lessons learnt

THE L42A1

The L42A1 rifle emerged from an already existing sniping rifle which had a very fine reputation hard won through years of continuous combat use. The L42A1 therefore had much to live up to, and it was largely successful in doing so. In its prime it certainly outperformed anything that had gone before it and it owed its improved accuracy to the very expensive match-grade barrel with which it was equipped. The L42A1 almost straight away found itself in the mêlée of Northern Ireland in the hands of skilled Royal Marines snipers who had learned their craft with the No. 4 Mk 1 (T), the L42A1's forebear. The early 1970s in Northern Ireland were lawless years, with violent gun battles breaking out on the streets, often prompting an emergency deployment of additional troops to the province.

The Royal Marines responded to the wave of armed violence with aggressive counter-sniper tactics employing the L42A1, which often involved snipers seeking out a derelict house, or a roof top. There they could secrete themselves away for several days and wait for an opportunity to present itself; and in those early years they did not have to wait for long. One former Royal Marine recalled his service in Northern Ireland in 1972, when Lieutenant-Colonel John Mottram, commanding officer 40 Commando, tasked his snipers with finding and occupying sniper hides in the New Lodge area of north Belfast. By the following year, the PIRA were so intimidated by the snipers' effectiveness that they curtailed their activities. In the absence of British Army sniper training, the veteran recalled, the Royal Marines were the only part of the British armed forces to train and deploy snipers in the early 1970s; only a handful of Army personnel were trained by the Royal Marines, and training places were limited.

It is fair to say that the PIRA had ambitious ideas regarding the use of their own snipers, who were simply outclassed and outgunned and found themselves very quickly out of their depth when they pitted themselves with inferior equipment against snipers of the Royal Marines and the British Army. Events during the first half of the 1970s led to the PIRA re-evaluating its use of gunmen, with emphasis being given to close ambush tactics; such events seemed to be randomly set up but of course that was rarely the case. The effective use of British Army and Royal Marines snipers armed with the L42A1 sniping rifle forced the PIRA commanders to adopt alternative tactics that helped expose the terrorists to other elements of the security forces. As a result, military sniping in Northern Ireland would never be as prolific in subsequent years, but the terrorist would continue to have a deep respect for the L42A1 rifle. When the L42A1 was deliberately presented routinely within a patrol group, its mere presence would be reported by Dickers, almost certainly thwarting attacks that were being prepared for that patrol. This was particularly the case in rural settings, where vehicle checkpoints were established on lanes or other country roads; soldiers operating these snap checkpoints were vulnerable and the presence of a sniping rifle made many terrorists think twice about launching an attack upon the security forces.

From the very beginning through to the end of its service life, the L42A1 would be dogged by forend and handguard issues that just would not go away. The rifle consumed them at a frightening rate as a result of the hard life it led; coupled with its thumping recoil, forends received heavy wear internally as well as sustaining external damage such as splits in the wood. A common issue with the forend and handguard involved the wood behind the stock band's rebated channel being elongated or chiselled away by the stock band itself when the sling was attached and then pulled heavily to assist a steady fire position. The repair involved the damaged area being cut away before new wood was glued and dowelled into place and then shaped to represent what was previously there. This repair could only be performed once, maybe twice, before the forend/handguard was written off.

There was a further issue concerning the front scope-mounting pad, which tended to work loose on heavily used rifles. The pads were originally fitted to a .303in rifle, which after conversion to 7.62mm calibre increased the pressure loading, resulting in a harsher recoil which could literally shake the three fixing screws loose. When this occurred it rendered the telescopic sight useless. In fact the L42A1's recoil would be a common theme running through the rifle's service life; it was not only responsible for the heavy wear on components, but also meant that the sniper had to be wary as the eye relief of the No. 32 L1A1 telescopic sight was very short. The L42A1 was unforgiving and would exact punishment on the user if not held correctly or if his concentration dropped, as the recoil would drive the rim of the scope tube into the sniper's face.

By 1980, just ten years into the L42A1's service, the No. 32 L1A1 telescopic sight was very quickly becoming the rifle's Achilles heel. By the mid-1980s, scope failure was the primary reason for an unserviceable rifle, with former snipers reporting that they did not keep the same rifle

A sniper from the early to mid-1980s with an L42A1 clad in green sniper tape. Note that the sling is a GPMG (general-purpose machine gun) sling clip-attached at the rear sling-swivel and slipped over the barrel with an improvised loop. Also note that the magazine is not attached, which suggests that the sniper is observing weapon-safety drills while practising. (Courtesy of the John Coffey Collection)

for more than a few months at a time. It is argued that it would have been cheaper and the units' use of the weapon would have been better served if the L42A1 had gone through an upgrade at about the ten-year point in its service life, rather than the perpetual stock repairs and command workshop attention it required through the last eight to ten years of its life. After all, even in 1970 the technology within the L42A1 was old and by 1972 the United States was moving away from the traditional rifle made of wood and metal, for this era saw the advent of composite stocks and synthetic bedding materials. The L42A1 would certainly have benefited from the upgrade of being synthetically bedded into a composite stock with an improved telescopic sight, evolving into the L42A2; instead, the rifle limped on into retirement, with most, if not all, L42A1s being withdrawn from service by 1988.

The L42A1 today is iconic, but it has to be said that its contribution to furthering and expanding the role of the sniper was minimal. The L42A1 never received the improvements perhaps that it should have throughout its service life and was therefore very quickly left behind in the technology stakes. Being very much a child of the 1960s, it was comparable in its construction to the American M40 sniping rifle as used in Vietnam, which of course did receive modifications and very quickly evolved into the M40A1 variant in the early 1970s. The L42A1 did, however, offer a tantalizing glimpse of how the sniping envelope could be extended beyond the British Army's doctrine of 600m 'lethal' and 800m 'harassing' ranges, in ways that harnessed the capabilities of most who passed through the six-week sniper course. So as not to judge the L42A1's reputation too harshly, it must be pointed out that in the hands of the most skilled, the rifle – equipped as it was with an excellent match-grade barrel – was capable of 900m 'lethal' accuracy, which in the early 1970s represented real progress. Snipers completing their training during the L42A1's service

life were the products of lessons learned back in World War II and Korea, however, and if indeed snipers from those wartime eras saw their successors of the 1970s and 1980s in action, they would have recognized their methods as being very familiar. Consequently, there were limitations and the L42A1 did not promote progression of the role, which stagnated for nearly 20 years with a platform that offered little versatility for additional accessories to be mounted, or for existing kit to be swapped out for better alternatives.

The L42A1 would be the last RSAF Enfield-produced sniping rifle to be fielded by the British Army; given this cachet, it has attracted a very strong following in the military-surplus rifle collector community, which has led to it being venerated by RSAF Enfield rifle enthusiasts. There have even been suggestions that the L42A1 was brought out of retirement to take part in the 1991 Gulf War, a claim yet to be substantiated; some are even convinced that the MoD placed orders for newly converted L42A1s as late as 2005. Whatever the truth to these claims, it is clear that the L42A1 has certainly touched the hearts of a great many rifle enthusiasts.

THE L96A1

The introduction of the L96A1 to British Army infantry units began in 1986; it was a staged affair, with units swapping their L42A1s for new L96A1s over a two-year period, only being briefly interrupted by the catastrophic failure of the latter's firing pin. There is little doubt that the innovative weapon that AI introduced to the world in the form of the L96A1 was ground-breaking: the designers had managed to break free of the mindset that a rifle's construction should involve a receiver being dropped into a stock and mechanically fixed in place – a monumental step forward.

For the first time, the British Army had adopted a rifle built solely for the job of sniping. The L96A1 was not simply a modified service rifle:

from the minute pencil touched paper on the drawing board, it was designed from a completely new perspective by people who were driven by the needs of competition shooting on the world stage. One of the radical features of the L96A1 was its consideration of ergonomics. It was a very comfortable rifle to shoot – the shooter and rifle naturally became as one – which, with its precision-engineered build, made for a robust weapon that would prove to be consistently deadly and completely dependable.

Regardless of the theatre of operations in which they served, British snipers were supremely confident with the L96A1 in their hands. One veteran recalled the massive increase in capability that occurred with the appearance of the L96A1, as snipers discovered that they could shoot with precision out to 600m and beyond; the introduction of more powerful optics and enhanced training pushed the range up to 900m and then 1,100m, an impressive jump given the properties of the 7.62mm calibre. He remembered the attachment many snipers felt to the L96A1 at the end of its 25-year service life, and praised the deadly accuracy of the rifle.

The L96A1 unambiguously heralded change; and it can boast another accolade: for a weapon to bring about a major revision of doctrine such as the increase of the standard 'lethal' and 'harassing' envelopes is not to be taken lightly. Practices as important as these are deeply embedded within the British Army and are not easily changed. Even so, the advantages the L96A1 brought to the sniper platoon could not be ignored; they were certainly not lost on Sniper Division, Warminster, leading to the first changes to *Pamphlet No. 4, Sniping*. The L96A1's robustness and long-range accuracy, packaged in a futuristic design, also allowed for a level of versatility never before seen. Different optics could be mounted and the weapon could be fitted with alternative accessories to accommodate additional equipment such as the revised forend block, which was redesigned to make the rifle STIC-compatible.

The L96A1 arrived in time for what would be an extremely active 20-plus years of service, immediately deploying as part of Operation *Banner* and thereby continuing the sniper's presence in both the rural and urban environments of Northern Ireland. The 1990s saw something of a resurgence of PIRA sniping in the rural areas of South Armagh after the PIRA terrorists acquired a .50-calibre Barrett rifle. Beginning in 1990, the PIRA had a number of opportunities to use this big-calibre weapon, which initially took the security forces by surprise. Incredibly, although this rifle was capable of extreme long-range the PIRA seldomly used it beyond 300m, with the terrorists' first eight attempts resulting in misses. It would take the PIRA two years to wound a soldier mortally, but the threat posed by the weapon was perceived to be far greater than the terrorists' abilities to shoot it; sooner or later they would get lucky again. Being first and foremost an anti-materiel weapon, the Barrett presented a threat to the Army Air Corps' helicopters, which routinely crisscrossed the South Armagh area.

The British Army responded to the threat posed by the Barrett rifle by sending an L96A1-armed sniper out with every 'brick', or patrol. In addition, each patrol also carried a GPMG to counter the threat. This response was hugely successful, with the PIRA's use of the Barrett rifle being reduced to what could be described as 'occasional' in comparison to the numerous brazen attacks the terrorists launched with the weapon on first acquiring it. In 1997, the PIRA's Barrett sniper team were cornered by the SAS after a Special Air Serviceman offered himself as a target to draw their fire. The Barrett sniper team fell for the lure by shooting at the SAS operative, who was moving around in the open and deliberately exposing himself to their fire. Unknown to the PIRA, the SAS man appearing to be making a multitude of mistakes and failing to make himself a 'hard target' was special forces and the opportunity proved to be irresistible. The shot the Barrett sniper team released missed, and in turn compromised their position to SAS teams that were waiting in the wings for the giveaway shot to help pinpoint the Barrett sniper team's location, which was subsequently stormed. The SAS operational brief was to capture, not kill; they were successful in this, capturing a four-man IRA team plus the Barrett rifle.

The Barrett rifle attacks were aided by a large PIRA support network, many of whom were 'Dickers' who drove around the area looking for British Army targets suitable for the Barrett sniper team to attack. The reported presence of an L96A1 in a patrol undoubtedly served to thwart potential PIRA attacks, particularly as the attacking distance was never any greater than 300m: over this distance, a British Army sniper armed with an L96A1 would have been devastatingly accurate – a point about which the PIRA men were only too aware.

The L96A1's illustrious career would include participation in Operation *Granby* (1991 Gulf War), Operation *Grapple* (Bosnia, 1992–95), KFOR (Kosovo, 1999 onwards), Operation *Barras* (Sierra Leone, 2000), Operation *Herrick* (Afghanistan, 2002–14) and Operation *Telic* (Iraq, 2003–11). The L96A1 spent a colossal amount of time fighting in two of the harshest environments on the planet – the Iraq and Afghanistan deserts – which offered searing heat, abrasive sand and fine powdery dust that entered almost everything. The L96A1 performed reliably, dispelling any ideas previously held that snipers had a very limited role in the desert because of environmental constraints on equipment. Although its Schmidt & Bender optic was also superlative, the upgraded L17A1 telescopic sight did develop an issue with its focus ring in the eyepiece, which became an entry point into its internal compartments for the fine powdery dust: this was rectified with an improved design of the component.

One veteran of the operations in Helmand, Afghanistan, recalled that his L96A1 remained completely reliable in combat, even in an ambush situation. As the ensuing firefight began, he opted to use his bipod and found a firing position; his spotter had to use his daysack as a rest for his 40× spotting scope. The pair quickly identified three potential firing points and one insurgent, only 125m away, firing from over some cover. Under cover of GPMG fire, the sniper shot the insurgent in the face; the spotter confirmed the kill and the sniper chambered another round. The spotter indicated another target some 300m away; although the sniper could see nothing at first, use of the 12× zoom allowed him to discern a

loophole and a gun muzzle within it. The sniper used a Mildot hold for speed and fired three rounds into the loophole, whereupon the firing ceased. He was subsequently credited with two kills.

A sniper pair armed with the L96A1 are pictured during a stalk; the routes of such stalks were frequently across very difficult terrain, as this pair demonstrate. The sniper will want to get to his firing point so he can settle into his 'sniper bubble'. (Courtesy of Chris Harrison)

Over its 25 years of service, the L96A1 acted as a bridge between traditional sniping tactics and a far more advanced use of the infantry's sniping asset, broadening the sniper's role to something that has become indispensable among battle planners. The role of the sniper today has increased significantly, but the tactics employed by snipers using the L115A3 did not suddenly appear in a new 'how to' pamphlet accompanying that weapon. Instead, they were pioneered by snipers armed with the L96A1; the versatility and the solid reliability of its accuracy – which provided a greater-than 85 per cent chance of striking a man-sized target out to 900m – have made routine such practices as coordinating multiple snipers in one operation.

Tasks were being performed with the L96A1 that would never have been possible with the weapon's predecessor – notably force protection, or the 'sniper umbrella' in sniper talk. Troops in Iraq and Afghanistan could operate in an area knowing that friendly snipers had commanding views of the ground, which instilled confidence in the troops who had to patrol in a less-than-welcoming neighbourhood. While threats on the ground could be dealt with by the troops themselves, however, the threat that was often lurking was at some distance from the ground, whether on a balcony, in an upper window or on a roof top. Such attackers were dealt with surgically by the sniper platoon acting in an overwatch capacity. This is just one example of how sniping practices have advanced and become structured and well-coordinated.

In the 1980s, the sniper and spotter trained to operate as a lonely pair, prowling the forward edge of the battlefield, gathering information and looking for priority targets; this is still true of the modern sniper, but the sniping rifle's evolving capabilities have made it possible to 'hunt as a pack', as was illustrated so brilliantly by snipers of 40 and 42 Commando of the Royal Marines during their 2003 assault on the oilfields on Iraq's al-Faw Peninsula. The Commandos' combined and coordinated use of L96A1-armed snipers was crucial to the success of the operation to prevent Iraqi forces destroying the oilfields as they withdrew. The Commando snipers acted as an attack force and cut-off group, and provided a 'sniper umbrella' as the main force swept through.

The L96A1 played a pivotal role in the development of the British sniper and how he does his job today. The weapon's futuristic design delivered something ground-breaking in the mid-1980s, back when even Sniper Division, Warminster could not have envisaged the far-reaching influence this rifle would eventually have on the sniper's war-fighting ability. Although the L96A1 has now long been retired, its battlefield impact has breached military boundaries and found its way into popular culture. It lives on in the gaming world and is also often the weapon of choice among Airsoft enthusiasts.

THE L115A3

British snipers on operations in Afghanistan began to receive the new .338in L115A3 rifle in 2008. It was immediately put to work alongside the L96A1, at which point the latter's withdrawal from service began. The L96A1's departure ushered in a new culture within British military sniping, one which promoted the wholesale buy-in of the belief that true long-range lethality had arrived. The essence of the L96A1 lived on in the L115A3 guise as the new weapon was also a chassis system, albeit much improved, and the weapon was still built with the very same principles of versatility and ease of maintenance in mind. By 2012, the L96A1 had disappeared from Afghanistan; but in its final days of service it was still being used in the sniper-training course as an intermediate step that the sniper student had to master before progressing to the large .338in calibre of the L115A3.

The L115A3 was well received: it delivered the same key benefits to which snipers had become accustomed with the L96A1, but those who witnessed the crossover from 7.62mm to .338in calibre instantly experienced incredible accuracy at an extended range previously unthinkable and unachievable by those of average ability. For the most skilled, the L115A3 was able to strike targets routinely out to 2,000m, and indeed in November 2009, just 12 months after the weapon arrived with snipers in Afghanistan, Corporal of Horse Craig Harrison of the Blues and Royals used an L115A3 to deliver his world-record shots on a Taliban machine-gun team at a staggering 2,475m. The L115A3 gave the British Army a real edge, day and night, with the use of both the SIMRAD and STIC. When it first arrived in theatre, the Taliban must have been utterly bewildered as to how they were

being targeted by effective rifle fire at distances they considered to be well out of range of British small-arms ground fire.

Snipers had always been a threat to the Taliban, but the increased threat the L115A3 brought to the battlefield made snipers a priority target. Patrols with a sniper openly carrying a 'long gun' drew an incredible amount of effort by the Taliban to eliminate the threat, leading to the L115A3 being delivered to a sniper or concealed in an improved carrying system as a means to deceive the Dickers.

An April 2010 British Army press release revealed how the L115A3's phenomenal accuracy allowed British forces to target insurgents without harming civilians in the vicinity. Marksmen of 1st Battalion, The Royal Welsh, tasked with covering bomb-disposal teams near Shahzad in Helmand Province, Afghanistan, were on patrol when they came under fire. The patrol quickly entered the compound that was their destination and their snipers immediately took up position on the roof. Their state-of-the-art optics allowed the Army snipers to win the firefight without any civilian casualties, despite the fact that the insurgents were using civilians as human shields; in some cases the insurgents were firing from loopholes, but the L115A3's accuracy allowed the Army snipers to target the insurgents successfully.

There is no doubt that the L115A3 sniping rifle has been a huge success and delivered the desired effect on a determined enemy. Their efforts to counter the L115A3's extended threat alone confirmed that its use hindered the Taliban physically and psychologically. The L115A3 has made engagement at extreme long ranges routine on the modern battlefield and has to some extent replaced expensive ordnance for the surgical

Soldiers of 3rd Battalion, The Parachute Regiment are pictured here operating in Helmand Province in August 2008. The rifle in the foreground is the L115A3, supplied in 2008 as part of the Sniper System Improvement Program. The weapon to the left is the venerable L96A1 rifle, which the L115A3 was set to replace over a four-year period. Note that the spotter is using a Leupold Mk 4 spotting scope; these were also supplied in 2008 as part of the SSIP. He is armed with an L85A2 assault rifle and a Glock 17 pistol. (Marco Di Lauro/Getty Images)

destruction of enemy combatants and/or their equipment. It could not be all things to all men in Afghanistan, however, with British Army commanders sometimes being blamed for poor deployment of the weapon system. The L115A3 was superlative in long-range engagements – and indeed that was exactly the role for which it was designed and introduced – but the combat environment in Afghanistan did not just feature open plains but also towns and villages where soldiers would very often find themselves in close-quarter combat. When such places were occupied, the L115A3 did not lend itself well to near-urban fighting involving very short engagement distances for which the rifle could not be brought to bear very quickly.

Where the L115A3 was deliberately deployed aggressively as part of a prepared firing solution in an operation which was likely intelligence-led, or when being used in 'sniper umbrella' operations, the rifle's deployment was exacting and its specialist attributes could be utilized to the full. It was sometimes a difficult weapon to apply effectively in the unassertive role, however, particularly in built-up zones in which sharpshooting outweighed the requirement for long-range precision fire.

The L115A3 and its AI antecedents owe a huge amount to the L96A1, which first emerged over 30 years ago and which along the way contributed substantially to the advancement of the sniping rifle itself as well as the development of sniping tactics.

THE AUTHOR'S APPRAISAL

My own military service and subsequent interest in the subject of British military sniping has from time to time brought me into contact with the three sniping rifles we are concerned with in this study, and I have indeed fired all three on numerous occasions over the years. It must be said, however, that I have not crawled on my belly for 100m taking advantage of the slight contours of ground to aid my concealment so as to arrive at a firing point undetected; nor have I walked into the kill zone of an enemy and been thrust into a vicious firefight with just seconds to account for myself with a sniping rifle; and I have never patrolled in searing 40°C heat, carrying a 'long gun' and presenting myself as a high-value target to my enemy. I have never fired the rifles featured here in any of these conditions like so many who have, and I am thankful for that. My experience with these rifles extends to a carefully manicured grassy firing point on a range with nothing more than a drizzly wet day and a few raindrops down my collar to discomfit me. For what it is worth, however, my observations are briefly as follows.

I have fired a number of L42A1 rifles, and I can say that although it was a privilege to do so, the L42A1 is a brute to fire. In my opinion, the best way to control the weapon is to use it in the 'Hawkins position', with the heel of the butt firmly dug in if possible, because the L42A1 loves nothing more than to punish fatigue or a drop in concentration by firmly hitting the shooter in the face on recoil. It is, though, capable of great accuracy: not in a target-rifle capacity delivering tight groups at 600m –

the telescopic sight will not allow it – but with the accuracy a sniper requires on a man-sized target. I have used the L42A1 out to 1,000yd (914m) with consistent hits on a Figure 11 target, as well as equally consistent shooting at a Figure 14 target at 600yd (549m). The L1A1 telescopic sight definitely impedes the L42A1's capability and the shooting experience is greatly improved with the L13A1 telescopic sight mounted.

It has been said moving to the L96A1 from the L42A1 is like going to a ray gun from a musket: it is indeed a very different experience. A precision-built rifle that offers incredible accuracy, the L96A1 is comfortable and (dare I say it) almost easy to shoot, whether off its own bipod, an improvised rest or the shooter's fist; it will drop rounds on a Figure 11 target at 800yd (732m) all day long and with the upgraded L17A1 telescopic sight mounted, it is

Dating from the 1970s, this is an original 20-round packaging box for the L2A2 ammunition manufactured at ROF Radway Green. The labelling specifies that the ammunition is for target use, with the label sporting the famous green spot by which the sniper-grade ammunition was best known. It was to accommodate this ammunition that the graticule lines on the L42A1's rear-sight slider were altered.

equally as capable at 1,000yd (914m). The L96A1 is not remotely in the 'brute' category, due to its excellent ergonomics coupled with the extra weight it has compared with the L42A1; the additional weight also possibly dampens the recoil slightly, given that both rifles use the same ammunition. After a morning on the firing point with this rifle it is easy to appreciate the L96A1's nickname, 'Green Meanie', and why it was much loved by the snipers who used it right up to the day it was retired from service.

As you would imagine, the L115A3 is a pleasure to shoot, employing as it does the same chassis system that the L96A1 introduced to the world. Being introduced to the L115A3 variant, however, means it would be easy to walk away thinking that the L115A3 rifle as a whole is something very special. The L115A3 is essentially the culmination of a decade of evolution, however, with the earlier L115A1 and L115A2 iterations having contributed improvements to the finished product; snipers who have used all three are quick to praise the L115A3 and its improvements, particularly with respect to the telescope, bipod, adjustable cheek rest and rear ground spike. I found the .338in Lapua round struck close (400m) targets with the power of Zeus, with little to no correction for wind necessary – yes, you read that correctly: 400m is close range for this supremely accurate rifle and its powerful 5–25×56 L24A1 telescopic sight. After the shorter-range targets were dealt with, the L115A3 was punching holes in Figure 12 targets at 1,200m with relative ease.

CONCLUSION

By April 1992, the L42A1 rifle was obsolete. Although its service would not officially end until the early 1990s, it actually began to be replaced after just 16 years in the hands of snipers. Furthermore, a great many of the rifles never fired a single round in anger, not in the L42A1 iteration at least. It is true to say of the L42A1 that it emerged at a juncture in the technology of the manufacture of bolt-action rifles; in 1970, when it entered service with the British Army, others were already exploring composite stocks and synthetic bedding materials, which proved to be hugely successful and would propel the manufacture of precision rifles going forward. In short, the L42A1 was lagging behind the innovative design and emerging technology that was emerging during its inception, which after just ten years of service was painfully obvious, with persistent breakages heralding the end.

The L42A1's retirement brought well over 100 years of the Enfield bolt-action rifles' service to a close. The period after 1992 saw the slow, bureaucratic matter of the weapons' disposal being shuffled from one MoD desk to another until finally, in 1994, the entire fleet of L42A1 rifles were deemed to be ready for disposal to the public through companies such as Navy Arms (in the United States) and Charnwood Ordnance (in Britain). To begin with, the L42A1s were sold as cheap military-surplus rifles with almost no value or status in the eyes of collectors; today, several reside in reference collections such as the Royal Armouries, Small Arms School Corps and Defence Academy of the United Kingdom museums, while other examples are sought after by private collectors across the world and change hands for impressive sums of money.

In the mid-1980s, the MoD had the choice of two replacement rifles for the L42A1. One option, the Parker-Hale M85, was equipped with a composite stock with a synthetically bedded receiver, but in the event Al's PM Rifle was selected and designated the L96A1. The weapon served

A British sniper is pictured taking aim with his L42A1 sniping rifle through thick woodland cover. He wears a handmade gillie smock which aids his concealment against the standing trees and undergrowth in a snowy winter landscape. (Courtesy of the John Coffey Collection)

with distinction in numerous conflicts, with many of its years of service involving combat use in unforgiving desert environments, the L96A1 largely owing its success to the revolutionary chassis system that lay at its heart. The L96A1 notched up over 25 years of service and was still involved in front-line sniping right up to the very day it was pulled from service in Afghanistan; it was given up sadly and reluctantly. Unlike the L42A1, it is possible that every L96A1 saw combat use, which is maybe why, with the exception of a handful of rifles, almost the entire 'Green Fleet' was destroyed in 2014–15; the lucky few that escaped destruction now reside in reference collections such as those held by AI and the Royal Armouries. At the time of writing, the L96A1 is quite possibly one of the rarest sniping rifles in the world.

Had events on the ground in Afghanistan been different and not dictated the adoption of a radically more capable sniping rifle, the 7.62mm calibre – and indeed the L96A1 rifle – might well still be current within the British Army. The L115A3 rifle is currently the British Army's sniper system, although elements such as special forces are using AI's AX rifle, which has already received the designation L115A4.

True to tradition within the British Army, special-forces personnel are often the first to receive such equipment and through their trialling and thorough evaluation the L115A4 will arrive with the field army in the optimal set-up for unit sniping use. Through special forces' use of the L115A4, the ammunition it uses is already one major factor likely to change when the weapon arrives with the field army. The ammunition is under scrutiny, with 300-grain (19.44g) bullets having been found to provide 100m of additional range when defeating targets such as body armour. When the transition happens, in or around 2030, the L115A3 receiver will undergo a transformation to L115A4 specification, as did the L115A1 and L115A2 receivers to L115A3 specification in 2007.

GLOSSARY

ADVANCE TO CONTACT A term applied to the action of moving forward towards the enemy until one is fired upon.

ANTI-MATERIEL A rifle platform in a calibre such as .50in BMG for the destruction of equipment or assets protected by armour or concrete with a range of bullet types for this purpose.

ARCS OF FIRE An area of ground in front of a fixed position in which the enemy is expected to appear. It is divided into 'corridors'; individuals are allocated a corridor of responsibility to cover with their weapons. Each corridor is overlapping so as to achieve interlocking fire.

BATTLEGROUP A single formation of all the fighting arms which supports one or more infantry battalions, generally including armoured regiments and artillery. More specialist elements can be allocated depending on operational requirements.

BOLT-ACTION The type of working parts possessed by a small arm. The term applies to weapons which have hand-operated working parts.

BOLT HOUSING CHAMBER The receiver of a bolt-action weapon has within it a chamber for the hand-operated bolt to be manipulated back and forth.

BRICK A term applied by British soldiers to a patrol body in Northern Ireland. A brick would normally consist of four men.

CES Complete Equipment Schedule; a set of items included as standard equipment with a weapon, or other device. The standardized items are usually packed with the principal piece of equipment and are considered to be essential to its use.

CHASSIS An alloy body on to which all other components, including the receiver, mechanically attach.

DICKERS Spotters or spies within the civilian population who are employed by the enemy to record one's movements and the types of weapons and equipment being carried.

DRUM Elevation or windage; the knobs or turrets on a telescope which carry the adjustment markings so the reticle within the telescopic sight can be physically altered to compensate for the bullet's flight trajectory.

ENGAGEMENT ENVELOPE The full extent of an area in which a weapon system is capable of delivering 'lethal' or 'harassing' fire on the enemy.

FLUTED BARREL A recess cut into the steel, usually found spaced around the entire circumference of a rifle barrel and which runs its full length.

FREE FLOATING BARREL A rifle barrel that has no support or contact with any other component along its entire length.

GPMG General-purpose machine gun; a belt-fed machine gun in 7.62mm calibre. Belgian in origin, it was introduced to the British Army in the 1950s. The weapon is still very much an important part of the British infantry section at the time of writing, providing a large percentage of the section's firepower.

'GREEN FLEET' A term applied collectively to all of the L96A1 sniping rifles.

'LONG GUN' A term given to a sniping rifle which is identifiable by being significantly longer than an assault weapon.

MOUNTING PADS Specially shaped steel blocks which are hand-fitted to the receiver wall for the precision positioning of an attachment.

PICATINNY RAIL A continuous metal rail which has been precision-machined into a repeating castellation. When a Picatinny rail is present on a weapon system it allows the attachment of any device or accessory equipped with a suitable mount.

RECEIVER A rifle's main body around which all other components attach to form the completed weapon.

RIFLING TWIST-RATE Indicates how many complete rotations the bullet will make as it travels along the rifle barrel.

SNIPER DOCTRINE Single standardized methods taught to all individuals connected with the activity of sniping, which unifies the employment of individuals who, once fully conversant, are deployable throughout the British Army.

SNIPER UMBRELLA A term given to the practice of snipers occupying elevated positions to provide precision covering fire for troops operating on the ground.

SRT The Scout Regiment Telescope.

SUPPRESSOR Often known as a moderator or silencer, this device attaches to the rifle barrel of a weapon and is used to reduce significantly the audible level of the weapon's report.

BIBLIOGRAPHY

Infantry Training Volume 1, Infantry Platoon Weapons Pamphlet No. 10, Sniping, 1951

User Handbook for the Rifles, 7.62mm, L42A1 & L39A1 and Telescopes, Straight, Sighting L1A1 & Scout Regiment, Land Service 1971

Infantry Training Volume 1, Infantry Platoon Weapons Pamphlet No. 10, Sniping, 1973

Sniper Pocket Book, 1973

Infantry Training Volume 1, Skill at Arms (Individual Training) Pamphlet No. 4, Sniping, 1976

Sniper Pocket Book, 1980

Infantry Training Volume 1, Skill at Arms (Individual Training) Supplement to Pamphlet No. 4, Sniping, 1986

Infantry Training Volume 1, Skill at Arms (Individual Training) Pamphlet No. 4, Sniping, 1990

Infantry Training Volume 1, Skill at Arms (Individual Training) Pamphlet No. 4, Sniping, 1996

Rifle, Sniper, 7.62mm, L96A1 Operating Information, 1996

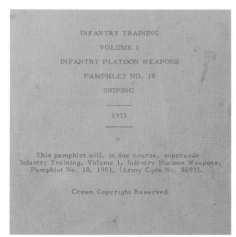

The 1973-dated pamphlet acted as a bridging pamphlet from the 1951 training literature, *Pamphlet No. 10*, to the 1976 purpose-written *Pamphlet No. 4*, which served the L42A1 for its entire service life, crossing over to the L96A1.

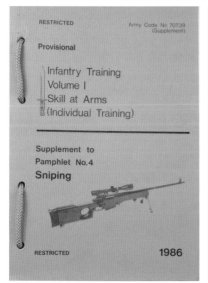
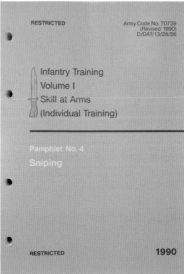

The 1976 *Pamphlet No. 4* was bridged by the 1986-dated supplementary pamphlet until 1990, when a purpose-written *Pamphlet No. 4* for the L96A1 was produced and circulated. A further *Pamphlet No. 4* was produced in 1996, which saw the L96A1 'Green Meanie' through to the end of its service life.

INDEX